Praise for

One Leaf in Time

"Sylvia Churchill Prince writes in a clear, readable way as she relates growing up in China, her years in a concentration camp, where she met the Sisters of Providence, to finally settling down in the United States. Cleverly interspersed in her memoir are the historical events that put her life experiences in perspective. How one person survived these ordeals makes for a fascinating read of *One Leaf in Time*."

—Sister Marie Grace Molloy, SP

One Leaf in Time

One Leaf in Time

A Memoir

By Sylvia Churchill Prince

BELLE ISLE BOOKS

www.belleislebooks.com

ISBN: 978-1-9399306-8-2

Library of Congress Control Number: 2015960174

Printed in the United States

Published by

BELLE ISLE BOOKS

www.belleislebooks.com

Dedicated to my little sister, Abigail, who was not with us in China and wanted to know more about our father, who died when she was only six years old.

ACKNOWLEDGEMENTS

With great appreciation to Dr. Laurence Mazzeno and my children for their patience, encouragement, and expertise in helping me with this memoir.

Photos of Massachusetts General Hospital loaned from their archives.

SOLILOQUY

An individual life can be compared to an aspen leaf falling into a trickling stream, where it is gently turned and cradled as it flows along with the current, to be carried with increasing speed, leaving behind the mother tree where it originated. It brushes against other leaves and twigs and is stopped occasionally by rocks, where it rests for a while before being swept back into the current. Then again, it may find an eddy where it will circle, not knowing its destination or worthiness . . . lost.

Finally, a nudge from a breath of wind will push it back to mainstream, where it will pummel over the rocks, twisted and beaten by gushing water, sometimes immersed, yet struggling to the surface with waning strength and fading color. Finally, brown and broken, it succumbs . . . decays.

This is the story of one leaf.

PREFACE

The 1800s were a century of tumult and adventure. Manifest Destiny, the fever that started after the settling of the American Colonies, was burgeoning with the increase of ships and transportation. Every country wanted to grab onto new possessions and land. Americans were not only expanding out west in a frantic "gold rush"; they were also building large wooden clipper ships, with three or four masts, that plied the ocean to the east and around Cape Horn to the West Indies and China, bringing back spices, silk, camphor, and tea to the Colonies.

Three of the docks in Plymouth, Massachusetts, were owned by members of the Churchill family, so Sylvanus Churchill, my great-great-grandfather, I believe, was an active merchant on the China Seas. He married Elizabeth Carver, and they had a girl named Abigail, who fell in love but didn't get married. The gold rush of the 1800s was enticing men to travel west and the gold bug bit her sweetheart. Off he went, sailing around the Horn to San Francisco, leaving poor Abigail pregnant in Plymouth. Thus, I am unable to discover the name or whereabouts of my great-grandfather.

Though she married Ozin Bates on September 4, 1871, it must have been terribly degrading for a woman of that day, living in a small Puritan town, to be carrying a child out of wedlock. When my grandfather, Harry West, was born, his birth was never recorded.

Harry, however, somehow received a good education and kept up the family tradition of trips to China for trade. In 1890, he was appointed Vice-Consul of Foochow, China, the walled capital of Fukien province, by James G. Blaine, secretary of state for the United States. Benjamin Harrison was president at that time.

In 1900, there was an uprising in China called the Boxer Rebellion. A Chinese secret society was formed to wipe out foreigners and their Western influences (such as Christianity), because their independence was being threatened. The Japanese had defeated China in 1895 and parts of China were under their control.

The Boxers, calling themselves "Patriotic Police," attacked foreigners and Chinese Christians in Tientsin and other large eastern towns. They went to Peking and murdered the German minister and the Japanese Chancellor. Two hundred thirty-one foreigners and many Chinese Christians lost their lives.

By August, troops from Austria, France, Germany, Great Britain, Italy, Russia, and the United States quelled the uprising, making the Chinese government promise to halt actions against foreigners. The Chinese also had to pay a total of $350 million to the countries involved.

Trading rights were guaranteed, in the form of the Open Door Policy. The countries reciprocated by returning some of the money and promising that no more arms would be brought into China. Foreign legations came back and each had their territory in the large cities called "concessions." Once again, history repeats itself as we battle today to claim our rights to oil in Iraq.

During this time, Grandfather Harry met and married a lovely young Malayan orphan who had been adopted by Baptist missionaries and educated at the University of California in Berkeley. Maili Thompson (her Christian name) had four children: Wilhelmina [Billie], Caroline [Carrie], Alice, and Thomas (my father). Although they grew up in Plymouth, they were all born in China.

Dad, born on July 27, 1894, started working for the Singer Manufacturing Company at the age of fifteen, but it was no surprise that on February 3, 1914, he went to the American consular service so he could obtain employment in Tientsin with an American firm. He started at the American Trading Corporation in 1912 at the age of eighteen, and so continued with them in China.

Born on the 21st of August, 1906, Ethel Lilly Lightfoot grew up in West Hartlepool, England. Her father, Alfred Henry Lightfoot, died at an early age and left his widow, Mary Ann Westgarth, to raise four children: Dolly, Tom and Hilda (twins), and Ethel. At times the widow took in washing; later she purchased a boarding house. Sometimes the guests were a little seedy, but she handled them.

Ethel, my mother, had a deformed right foot and, as the family was quite poor, never had it operated on. Nevertheless, she did not let it hamper her.

During World War I, the Germans bombed Hartlepool unmercifully, and Ethel and her family had to rush to the basement as the air raid sirens announced the approach of German zeppelins and bombers. Her cat prophesied the air raids by hiding under the kitchen table long before the blast of sirens. The zeppelins were able to fly 10,000 feet in the air, so they were hard to detect. Bunkers were built along the shoreline and they remain there today as an epitaph. The Germans also bombed towns such as Berwick and Tweed in the north and Warrington and Birmingham in the west.

London, however, was always the Germans' prime target. On September 7, 1940, at the start of World War II, German bombers followed the Thames River to find London and succeeded, even though the city was blacked out. They bombed many major buildings, such as Ten Downing Street and Buckingham Palace. Thousands of British citizens were killed, and several buildings and cathedrals were burned out.

CHAPTER 1
ROOTS

Gently he wrapped the front of his battered field coat around me, pulling me closer to his chest. "The wind is getting kinda cold, Sylvia," the lanky marine whispered into my auburn hair. His muscular arms reached out, around me, to grasp the ship's rail and give me protection from the weather.

We were on the deck of the USS *Lavaca*, a troop transport ship, bound for San Francisco, and I had dreams of a new life—a fabulous adventure. The thought of it made me shiver more than the cold. How would we survive?

So many things had happened in my short eleven years to bring me to this moment, standing at the rail of a lurching ship in the arms of an Okinawa marine. As I watched the rise and swell of the granite waves and the foaming white wake I couldn't help thinking of the life I was to leave behind and the one I would encounter in America.

A short, sinewy man with the typical thin lips and smooth black hair of his Asian ancestry, Dad strode with the air of a man of importance. Totally disciplined, he had taught himself algebra and the use of the abacus, an instrument made up of beads strung on wood dowels, on which one could perform calculations in large numbers.

His father, who had been Vice-Consul of Foochow, China, influenced Dad to seek a sales position in the American Trading Company. It was based in Tientsin, but on one of his sales trips he was sent to London, England.

"What is your name? Ethel?" She was quite a head-turner, with a peaches-and-cream complexion, sitting behind the cashier's desk at Lyle's restaurant. Her forget-me-not blue eyes and wispy brown bangs soon won his heart, and it wasn't long before he was asking the hand of this gutsy English lass.

Though just twenty-four, Mom, very much in love, waved goodbye to her family and homeland. She must have had sorrowful feelings as she kissed her brother and two sisters farewell. In her hand, a suitcase contained a few belongings and a leather boot that she used for her congenitally deformed foot. (She was able to walk better and even danced with this prosthesis laced up to the knee. At that time the waltz and ragtime were quite popular. In the Grand Palace in New York, people were dancing in contests that lasted for days. Mom enjoyed keeping up with the times.)

"Tom has a beautiful home in Tientsin, China, and will meet me in Moscow," she told her mother. Mary Westgarth Lightfoot accompanied her daughter across the English Channel on the USS *America*, kissed her goodbye, put her on the Trans-Siberian Railway (built in 1892 by the Russian czars), and let her go. She would not see her youngest daughter again until long after the war. When Mother went back to England in 1957, grandmother was senile and in a nursing home.

The Trans-Siberian Railway from Hamburg, Germany, cost about forty-eight pounds. Conditions were poor on the train. There was no food served, so Mother had to rely on short rations of biscuits and tea, which she warmed on a kerosene burner. Mother's trip took place during the war between Russia and China over boundaries, so at every stop Russian military boarded the train and searched the passengers.

"Open your suitcase!" the burly, ruddy-faced lieutenant demanded. Mother had packed light, hoping to buy her trousseau when she reached Moscow. "What is this? Look here!" he called to his comrades, holding up Mother's leather boot with the laces trailing. The soldier could not contain himself. "Look at this!" Dancing with the boot as if it were a false leg gone awry, he pranced around the compartment. They all thought it hilarious and burst into raucous laughter. Mother was overwhelmed with embarrassment. Her cheeks blazing, she snatched the boot out of the soldier's hands, threw it back into the suitcase, and slammed down the lid. With eyes flashing, Mother defied the soldier to advance upon her. He retreated and left her cubicle in a hurry.

When Mother arrived in Moscow, my father was waiting as promised. We couldn't help wonder, "What if he hadn't been there?" After a wonderful evening of dining and dancing all night, they continued on the Trans-Siberian Railway, crossing through Siberia, Mongolia, and around the Gobi Desert. Cutting through the Great Wall of China, the train proceeded on to Tientsin.

A big wedding ceremony was held at the house on Race Course Road in Tientsin. Most of Dad's relatives were there, although his father had died earlier of tuberculosis. Dad's mother and sisters were living with him. It bothered Mother that there was no one there to represent her or even give her away. A friend of Dad's had to do the honors.

"Take big breath! Push!" Two Japanese midwives assisted Mom's delivery at the house when I was born. It was May 4, 1934. At the same time, passing through the Panama Canal, President Franklin D. Roosevelt viewed the main U.S. fleet, America's naval strength. Who knew this fleet would be so inadequate for the battle that was to come?

"Come here and see your new sister," Dad called to my two older brothers. Tom, born in 1931, was three, and Harry, born on October 24, 1932, was just eighteen months old. After counting all my fingers and toes, they asked, "What's her name?" Sylvia was a name used in one of the songs of the day ("What Is Sylvia, Who Is She?"). "Sylvia," Dad said, "and her middle name is Mary. She is named after her grandmother." It didn't seem to impress the boys. "Oh," they said. "We were hoping for a brother."

Chapter 2
THE "WILLOWS"

The Georgian-style house built by Dad's father (Harry) was sandwiched between a dairy and peasant huts on Race Course Road. It had several gardens and two small ponds encircled by willow trees; hence, it was called "The Willows." A brick wall, seven feet tall, enclosed the property. Dad purposely had it studded with all colors of broken glass to keep out thieves.

A large club was at the end of Race Course Road. Dad and his cronies would bet on the horses, swim, and play tennis there. In his study, tennis trophies were proudly displayed on a shelf. He was an excellent tennis player.

Our brick house stood on a four-foot high terraced mound with a drive-under garage in the back. It was four stories high, including the attic where I played with wood blocks left over from the building of the house.

The third floor held two baths and four bedrooms. One room was occupied by my aunt Carrie, the other room, near the front, was Grandma's.

I remember my grandmother well: a tiny, withdrawn, and gentle woman with jet-black hair neatly pulled back in a bun. Her olive skin, from Malaya ancestry, was always soft and supple, with just enough coloring to the lips and cheeks. A large black beauty spot, which I inherited, dotted the right side of her face over her upper lip. She spoke perfect English.

It was a real treat to be invited into her unusual bedroom, with its beautiful silk bedspread and plush green Oriental rug. She would show me her trinkets and Chinese jewelry. There were hand-carved ivory elephants, jade and pearl necklaces that she draped around my neck, and red silk slippers to adorn my feet. Somehow, I felt an inner peace while chatting with her.

Whether she was ostracized by the family or preferred to be alone, I never really knew, but Grandma spent most of her time in the confines of her room, reading or doing handwork. She wasn't put in the prison camp with the rest of us, and we really never knew what had become of her until we were liberated and sent to the United States. Connie White, her goddaughter, sent us word that she had been living in an apartment, raising chickens, in Tientsin. She died without her family near; only one of her Chinese friends was at her bedside.

At the bottom of our house's large spiral staircase, there was a living room to the right, and a dining room to the left adjoined by a formal foyer. In the back, Dad had a library where he displayed his gun collection. Shelves were covered with books and trophies and an old Phillips radio. The radio kept him abreast of news around the world, and we were given strict orders not to touch it.

Farther down, a large pantry was stocked with condiments and canned goods. From this room, "Boy," as we called him, would reach through the back of the dumbwaiter to arrange the meal. The dumbwaiter was a four-foot square wooden tray lifted by pulleys from the basement kitchen up to our formal dining room. Two cabinet doors concealed it between meals.

Boy was Dad's personal butler. Not like the usual short Chinese, he was almost six feet tall and had light hair and gray-blue eyes. With quiet demeanor, he would press and set out clothes for Dad and take care of the housecleaning. Unlike Da Nang, our cook, he rarely smiled or chuckled at our antics, but whenever you entered a room, he was there. Whenever we needed tea served or to be entertained, Boy had it under control. He was the main cog in the working of the house, and though he never got close to anyone, we all felt his genuine loyalty. When we had dinner, Boy would stand behind my chair and cut up my food after he'd waited on the table.

Tom, Harry, and I would play hide-and-seek in the evenings under the large dinner table while the fireplace cast shadows into the room.

One of the rooms in the basement was a bedroom for the Amah, the woman who cleaned and looked after the children in our house. Taking a peek inside one day, I was fascinated with the starkness and somber surroundings. Her red velvet neck-roll sat on one end of a flat, smooth bed with no mattress, while a small dressing table held a tortoise-shell brush and comb. An old wooden chair and woven cotton rug were the only other furnishings. On the walls hung Oriental pictures with red tassels, their unframed silk highlighted with bold colors. (The Chinese equate the color red with good luck and prosperity.)

The kitchen was located directly under the dining room so that the freshly cooked meal could be placed in the dumbwaiter. Da Nang, the cook, presided over this room with its centered, long, butcher-block table and bank of large ovens over a huge wood stove.

"Tiffin" was served at noon and high tea was frequently served at four o'clock. We enjoyed having high tea with scones, jam and cream pastries, and chocolate éclairs. The boys and I had to sit at a separate small table because Dad always invited friends, plus my aunts and Grandma. We would sip our tea from our English bone china teacups and pretend we were so grown up!

Da Nang had been trained by my grandfather to cook American dishes. He was Cantonese, but his apple pie and pot roast were to die for. When I wandered into his domain, like a Kung Fu artist he would pick up his large butcher knife, and with fake viciousness would chase me out, wielding it over his head. Then, with a few more kicks of his feet, he would return to his lair, chuckling under his breath. It was a bizarre game, but I enjoyed it.

In the laundry room next to the kitchen, I remember helping the second Amah roll dough and fill "chowsers" with ground beef, pork, and either spinach or cabbage. They were made with a pastry of flour water and sesame oil cut into circles. She worked with precision and speed, wetting the edges with water and folding over and pinching them just enough to keep the dumplings from opening in the boiling chicken broth. In no time, a hundred to two hundred three-inch chowsers were lined up on the flour-dusted table. And were they good!

In the garage next to the kitchen, a beautiful new Rolls Royce was housed. A driveway cut through the terraced area at the back of the house. The driveway circled to the front and out the main gate. Also in the basement, Dad had a workroom where he planned his inventions. One of his designs was a rickshaw that would not have to be pulled by a coolie but could be pushed from behind by a bicycle. It made it so much easier for the driver to pedal rather than pull his client—often in homemade sandals and drenched in sweat. The passenger also found it pleasant to see the scenery instead of the back of a bamboo hat.

Common knowledge had it that you never agreed to the price first charged by the rickshaw driver. Instead, you had to haggle with the driver while he walked along with you, sometimes reaching your destination before settling on a price.

Dad also carved a lot of planes, cars, and boats, all with movable parts. He had the latest lathes and equipment, and we had a closet full of lovely wooden toys to play with.

A large glass conservatory was connected to the living room of our house. "Let me water the plants, Mother," I would beg, and she would accompany me into the jungle of rubber plants, ficus, and ferns. I loved to draw pictures on the moist glass windows and breathe the pungent, fertile air.

Parties were held frequently at my parents' friends' homes and Mom loved to go, but Dad often left her home. Throwing his dancing shoes over a shoulder, he would kiss me goodbye, rumple the boys' hair, and speed off in the Rolls. Mother was very outgoing and popular with the men, which made Dad jealous. Even with her bad leg, she would get out on the ballroom floor in her beaded satin dress and bangle-covered arms. Her bright blue eyes sparkling from a frame of tight brown curls, she could execute the Charleston, Turkey Trot, or the Lambeth Walk, which ended with a thumbs-back gesture, and, with much gusto, a loud "Hey!" Watching Mom practice in the living room was fun, but no matter how I tried, my legs and knees would go in different directions and I would get all tangled up on the floor. (So much for the Charleston.)

One time a German officer danced with Mom all night and the next day sent her an enormous box of chocolates in the shape of a large, red heart. It was as big as a hula-hoop and covered with lace and red roses. We were all looking forward to sampling those chocolates, but Dad refused to let Mom open them and they remained in the refrigerator until they got moldy and were thrown out.

"Get me my guns," Dad would call to the servants. "I'm going duck hunting today, so tell Da Nang not to prepare any dinner tonight." Taking a couple of the servants and one of the dogs, Dad would spend the day in the reeds and rushes of the main canal. Usually he came home with five or six birds in hand for Da Nang to cook.

There were always a lot of dogs at our house because Dad loved to breed and train them. One time it was Irish setters with beautiful red coats that gleamed in the sun. Another time he raised a family of German police dogs. And then there was Mickey, a lop-eared Airedale with bristly chin, who was our pet. Mickey followed me everywhere. He was so gentle, we could climb all over him and he'd wag his tail and nuzzle us. Then we found out that if we lifted his tail a little gas would escape. How we tormented that dog! It made us roll over laughing and each one of us had to have a try.

In this luxurious setting we lived like kings. A hymn written by Isaac Watts in the 1700s states, "See how we trifle here below, fond of the Earthly toys." It was the good life.

One Leaf in Time

Grandpa Harry as Vice Consul of Foochow

DEPARTMENT OF STATE,

To all to whom these Presents shall come, Greeting:

I Certify That *Harry W. Churchill, of Massachusetts,* has been appointed *Vice Consul* of the United States at *Foo-Chow,* with all the privileges and authorities of right appertaining to that office, subject to the conditions prescribed by law. In testimony whereof, I, *James G. Blaine,* Secretary of State of the United States, have hereunto subscribed my name and caused the seal of the Department of State to be affixed.

Done at the City of Washington this *26th* day of *November,* in the year of our Lord one thousand eight hundred and *ninety,* and the *115th* year of the Independence of the United States of America.

Charles Denby

Document signed by George Blaine

CHAPTER 3
SCHOOL AND SUCH

Tom and Harry attended the Saint Joseph's College for Boys, run by Franciscan Brothers in Tientsin. Every morning they would jump on their bicycles, dressed in shirts and ties, and ride about three miles to school. When they came home at four o'clock, they had homework to do. I remember Tom staying up late one night, memorizing the catechism while he paced through the house. It must have been past midnight.

Girls were not allowed to go to school, so I was homeschooled, which suited me fine! The stories the boys brought back about being whipped and caned for any breech of school rules really frightened me, and I was thankful I didn't have to face such an ordeal. Instead, Mother taught me spelling and reading and Dad introduced me to arithmetic. Each morning Mom would give me a list of spelling words. After I had memorized them, she would call them out to me, and each time I spelled one wrong, I would get a crack across the knuckles with her ebony ruler. It wasn't long before I became a pretty good speller.

"Hit him, hit him!" Dad would shout. "Keep your left up, Harry. Jab with your right, Tom!" As young as nine or ten, Dad would put boxing gloves (big as the boys' heads) on them and make them fight until the tears were streaming down their cheeks and blood was running from their noses.

Mother and I would stand in a corner of the living room and cringe as the boys "duked it out," their hair dripping and faces beet red, too afraid of their father to quit. Finally Mother would shout, "That's enough, Tom! Stop it." Then Dad would let the boys take off their boxing gloves and shake hands. Who knows, when Tom went into the Marines and Harry joined the Army, whether this training may have helped them. Tom had a grueling training at boot camp in Cherry Point. Growing up, the boys were inseparable and even went on double dates together. They live close to each other today.

One Leaf in Time

While I was a baby, Mom often read to me and Dad would sing the songs of the day while he paced the floor with me in his arms. He liked excerpts from Gilbert and Sullivan's *Mikado*. Poor Butterfly, though, she kept on waiting. It still brings tears to my eyes.

When I was sick with chicken pox, scarlet fever, and whooping cough, Mother would sit by my bed for hours and read me the Little William stories. Little William was always getting into trouble like Tom Sawyer, but unlike Tom, his anecdotes were in England, where he would end up falling into a stream, ripping his britches, or trampling a lovely flower garden. "Read me some more about Little William, please, Momsie," I would plead between the horrible gasps of whooping cough.

When I was feeling better, Mom would let me play with the boys' lead soldiers. The wonderfully festooned brigadiers and red-coated foot soldiers would hide in the folds of the blanket and shoot at each other. Soon I would encounter the throes of war and soldiers, but these would be dressed in dull khaki and carry real guns.

The remarkable thing about this house was that it was haunted. On its site once stood an emperor's palace, and evidently his daughter fell in love with the son of a feudal enemy. Anyway, when her parents refused to let them wed, the princess reportedly hanged herself in despair (just like the story of Romeo and Juliet).

Dad was coming in the front door one day, shortly after the house was built, and saw a beautiful young lady, dressed all in white, standing at the top of the staircase. He was accustomed to visitors just dropping in for a visit, so he advanced to the stairway with a cheery, "Hello, who are you?" The girl fluttered down the stairs and, at the end of the stairwell, vanished!

A noose framed in the transom of my aunt's bedroom door could be seen in the evenings on certain nights. Tom and Harry would coax me to accompany them up the stairs when we went to bed and I would nonchalantly lead the way. It made me proud to be the "brave guy," even though I was just as frightened. As soon as we climbed the stairs, we would dash into our bedroom and slam the door. Aunt Carrie didn't seem bothered by the "ghost" in her bedroom, and she spent many days shopping for silk garments in Canton anyway.

The gardens around the house were kept groomed by two gardeners. Banks of pink, white, red and yellow hollyhocks lined the paths, which led to different areas. Centered between the paths, a large stone fountain surrounded a cone of coke cinders about eight feet tall. As it was usually dry, I would jump down into the fountain and play with the porcelain figures glued into the grooves of the colorful cinders. In each niche Dad had placed trees, temples and people so that they were living on the sides of the rocky cone. It reminds me now of the houses built on the lava beds in Hawaii. When the fountain was activated, water spewed down the cinders and flowed under little bridges with Chinese ladies and men on them. I loved my big dollhouse.

Edging the terrace around the house, a brick planter held portulaca, snapdragons and marigolds. But the most enjoyable area was our playground. Along the sides of this fifty-foot strip, old wine bottles, buried deep, bordered rows of four-o'clocks, marigolds, zinnias and cock's comb. The fragrance of jasmine filled the air.

The playground contained a tall swing set and slide. Down at the farthest end stood an eight-sided pigeon cote, and behind the playground, a huge tree in which Dad had built a playhouse with a suspended rope ladder. A path from the play area led down to the garden and little farm that were bordered by one of the ponds. There, Dad grew corn, tomatoes, beans, cabbage and sugar cane. He also raised goats, pigs, and chickens. The goats gave us milk every day and the chickens provided eggs and meat.

In the play area, the boys and I would push each other on the roof-high swings. "Higher!" I'd shout, and soon, the wind blowing through my long hair and taking my breath away, I could see over the wall the thatched huts and countryside of the world I was not able to enter.

CHAPTER 4

NATURE'S FURY

As we were located near the Mongolian border, we were pelted one year with a sandstorm from the Gobi Desert. It was late in the morning when the sky turned a viscous gray-yellow. I was playing among the hollyhocks, and being very small I had no comprehension of what was to occur. Intrigued, I watched as the servants dashed around the outside of the house, slamming the heavy wood shutters over every window and bringing in porch furniture and pots.

Amah let out a scream and dashed out to get me just as the sand started swirling and stinging my eyes. She grabbed my hand, muttering something in Chinese (I believe I heard Boy say the same words when he dropped something in the parlor), and whisked me into the house. Tom and Harry were at school, so I had no one to share the experience of hearing the "swoosh" of sand against the house and hail-like tapping as it hit the windows. Though the sandstorm only lasted a day, it covered all the gardens and porch, leaving the servants to sweep up sand for a long time.

Years later, when my son, John was in Iraq, I understood what he was going through when he wrote that he woke up with two inches of sand on his body each morning.

Nature took another turn at the house when I was about four. The Great Flood of 1939 devastated the whole area. Dad had just started his garden again and purchased some new livestock. Every fall he slaughtered a pig. Though I hated to hear the squeals and death gasps, plugging my ears as he slit their throats, the bacon and pork chops were mighty good. Tom, Harry and I would fight over the heel of French bread so we could stuff it with bacon and munch away.

We were finishing lunch (which we called *tiffin*). Boy had cut round sweet watermelons in half and we each devoured one—they were so delicious! A farmer came by every day with his handcart piled high with the dark, green, soccer-size fruit and only charged twenty-five cents for them.

With our bellies full, we marched upstairs for our afternoon nap. As Tom passed the bedroom window, he stopped short. "Harry, Sylvia. Come here and see this. There is something happening outside!" he shouted.

We rushed to the window and, standing on our tiptoes to see over the windowsill, looked out to where we heard excited voices outside. Dad, Boy, and the gardener walked abreast from the garden. Filling up the landscape behind them, as far as the eye could see, was a mantle of shining water. Slowly it crept around tree and building, filling in every crevice and hole like a gigantic gray Pac-Man gobbling up the land. Steadily it came, wave upon wave, rising higher and higher, over the ponds, the gardens, our playfield, and around the house.

Some said that the flood was caused by a warlord who dammed up the Yellow River so he could punish his neighboring adversary. Others prophesied that the river would overflow every thirteen years. (As we were not there the next thirteen years, I cannot verify this.) Some said the Chinese dammed the river to keep the Japanese from crossing it and devastating their towns in the southern regions. Whichever, there were thousands of Chinese peasants and livestock drowned.

All night long we could hear the mournful mooing of the cows in the dairy next door and their slapping and splashing in the murky water. Next morning, the bodies of horses floated by, their bellies bloated and draped with debris.

One day, floating by our window was the body of a well-dressed Chinese lady. On her chest, oblivious to the fact that he was riding a corpse, sat a big green frog. It made my stomach turn, but it was hard for me to take my eyes away as I watched her body float by. Being only four years old, it was a traumatic ordeal to be introduced so rudely to death, and my heart goes out to the little children of the Middle East who are being subjected to such horrible sights during the wars there.

The servants had moved everything up to the second floor of the house, which luckily was raised an extra four feet due to the terrace around it. Unhappily, the delicious squab that Da Nang had prepared in the kitchen was wasted.

Some of the servants moved to the pantry area and the chickens occupied the living room on our rolled-up, thick, white Oriental rug. They were quite a sight perched on the piano, rug and chairs.

Somehow the pigs survived, possibly on the greenhouse roof. When the flood finally subsided after three months, they appeared on the terraced area and fed on water moccasins. Running around the corner of the house one day, I came upon three of the muddy animals and there was one of the pigs with a two-foot length of snake wiggling down his throat. It was grotesque!

Though we seemed to get enough food, there were a lot of complications brought on by the flood. Dad had to climb out the living-room window and paddle a canoe to work. He was trying to save the business records of the Dunlop Company where he started employment in 1934. Tientsin was also flooded, as the waters stretched for miles, and while wading through waist-high putrid water, he stepped on a rusty nail.

In China, any penetration of the skin was a dangerous thing. Bacteria covered everything and tetanus was a common killer. Dad, with his leg bandaged and suspended in a sling from the bottom of the bed, lay in a fever for weeks. Watching Mother and the servants fanning him, I thought surely he would die. There were no antibiotics in that day, so gentian violet, iodine, and alcohol were the only medications available.

Finally, Dad got well, but it took a toll on his health. He never played tennis again and remained gaunt the rest of his life.

"Where do you want me to pole this thing?" Harry's voice was edgy. He didn't want to take our makeshift raft out into the murky, germ-filled water, but I had a way of bossing him. He was always so good-natured, I usually got my way, and we had been confined to the house for two months, so he was ready to venture out, too.

Sitting gingerly on the rotten pieces of foraged board, we poled ourselves out over what used to be the front yard. "Go over there!" I demanded, seeing something floating in the water. With a sigh, Harry took a pole, which was only about six feet long, and pushed over to the spot. Suddenly, his face turned white as a sheet. "I can't reach the bottom!" On his knees, he tried to extend the pole up to his armpits but just couldn't touch the ground.

We were stuck! Evidently the area I had made my poor brother pole to was over one of the ponds. "What are we going to do, Harry? We might be marooned on this raft until nighttime," I moaned in fear.

"Let's try using our hands, we'll get back," consoled Harry. Kneeling on either side of the raft, we paddled frantically. It was nasty having to get our hands in the smelly water, but little by little we maneuvered our flimsy craft back to the living-room window and safety. Boy, did we get a lecture that night and, as usual, Harry got blamed for taking his sister out.

Gradually, the water receded. The gardens were a mess and Dad's Rolls Royce had to be junked. For sentimental reasons, he saved one of the front seats and placed it in the corner of the dining room.

"You're peeking!" Tom called out as we were playing hide-and-seek. The old car seat had become our favorite place to be "it" and I was leaning over the back of it to hide my face. Trying to lean further, I made it tip backwards, throwing me onto a steam-heat radiator and gashing my forehead on one of the ridges.

Dad rushed me, spewing blood, into his library and tilted me back in his big leather chair. Of course I must have been screaming my head off I was so terrified. Out came the gentian violet, which he poured into the wound. Then he applied a sterile bandage, which he wrapped tightly, like a turban, around my head. The bandage stayed on for several weeks and every time I entered the house, I would try to pull it off, thinking it was a hat. My forehead still has the scar.

The sky was black with them. Sounding like steam coming from a hot iron, locusts swarmed one afternoon. The sky was so full of these brown-bodied pests that none of the horizon was discernible.

Dad had just replanted the garden after the flood. Vegetables, sweet corn, and sugarcane were growing tall, and green leaves were returning to the willows, elms, and mimosa trees.

Resembling large grasshoppers, these ravenous insects devoured everything in sight! Sometimes they covered a stalk of corn or blade of grass so completely that you could only see their shiny, speckled bodies and fluttering wings. In an hour they were gone, migrating on to the next area, leaving a swath of ravaged land behind, completely devoid of vegetation or greenery.

The poor farmers around us lost all of their crops, too, and starved during the winter months. Dad never did recover much of his vegetable garden after that and had to import food from Peking.

Chapter 5
SWEET MEMORIES AND DARK CLOUDS

As soon as I was able to toddle, Mother took us to church in Tientsin. I dreaded attending this huge Episcopal church. About twenty large stone steps led up to this gray granite cathedral. Inside, it smelled musty, and the kneeling benches, which Mother insisted we kneel on, were bare wood. Very hard for small knees!

Dad would press a nickel into our hands and wish us well, but he never attended. How I wished I could remain at home with him instead of having to face the dark, bearded minister with his heavy robes, who reminded me of the giant in "Jack and the Beanstalk."

Then one Easter, he approached me after the service and said, "I'd like to show you something, Sylvia." Reaching for my hand with a large paw, he almost had to drag me around to the back of the church. There, a hutch made of chicken wire stood, with two pink-eyed bunnies nibbling grass inside. "These rabbits symbolize why Jesus died on the cross," the giant of a man explained. Gently he reached into the hutch and lifted a rabbit out by the scruff of its neck. Then he tucked it into my eager arms. "He wanted us all to start new without the burden of our sins, and live with love, hope, and softness in our hearts," the Reverend continued. "Just like these soft new rabbits."

I do not recall the name of the church or the minister, who was so strong and yet so tender, but what he said and the feel of the soft innocent bunny that snuggled into my warm sweater will stay with me forever. When I walk into church now, I feel at home.

It was May 4th, I must have been five, and how I anticipated this day with excitement. Jumping from under the hollyhock-embroidered coverlet, I raced to get dressed and be welcomed with cheers of "Happy Birthday!" To my surprise, everyone acted normally and all through breakfast there was not a mention. The boys soon rode off on their bicycles to school and Mom plaited my hair, but still no mention of my special day.

I wanted so badly to remind them, but then I thought, "They must be planning a surprise party, why spoil it?" Afternoon came and waned and there was no cake from Keiserlings, the German pastry shop that supplied our goodies. Mom was sitting and knitting in the parlor and Dad called to say he would be late. "Could they have forgotten me?" I ran to my room very depressed and sobbed in my pillow.

Dad usually took us into town in a rickshaw on our birthdays and we got to pick out a little present in the big Tientsin department store. (One year I wanted a toy piano so badly but Dad thought it silly so he got me a wooden puzzle that made up into a small table and two chairs, and was I disappointed!)

Anyway, about 5:00 p.m., there was a scramble at the front door and there stood my two aunts. Aunt Carrie held a beautiful porcelain doll with golden curls and a gold bobby pin in her hair and Aunt Alice pushed in a wicker baby carriage with all the trappings. They also carried a dozen colorful ribbons tied to balloons for my hair. Although my parents felt bad, it was the best birthday I'd ever had.

Dad was sometimes quite cruel with his attempts at discipline. One day, when I was about three, I was upset at Mother, who was trying to comb knots from my long hair. "Go to Hell!" I blurted out. Goodness knows where I had heard that, but Dad was called and I was placed over his knees and paddled severely. Poor Amah was so upset as she stood me on a table and examined the redness of my bottom. "Huai Ren, Huai Ren," she muttered. It meant "Bad man, bad man." The amahs were always taking good care of us. One kept trying to get me to eat more and I learned my first words of Chinese, "Chi Bao La," meaning "I'm full."

The Grand Canal, built by Yang Jian, stretched 1,100 miles in several directions and was used as a waterway for peasants to travel with their goods to markets in the cities, such as Peking, Tsingtao, Shanghai, and Tientsin. It also served as an irrigation canal.

One Leaf in Time

The weather in Tientsin could be bitterly cold with snow freezing into ice encrusting the land, then alternately melting and refreezing again. During the colder months of winter, the Grand Canal would freeze over and coolies could skate on it pushing a sled with wooden poles. Snug in fur robes, with only our noses exposed to the freezing wind, we slid with ease along the canal. Three people could fit comfortably and ride for miles. What fun!

One day we were visiting my aunt in the city. It had snowed and frozen into icicles that looked like stalagmites sticking out of the ground. Harry and I decided to throw snowballs at each other. Out we went. Harry found a huge chunk of ice and started chasing me with it. "You can't catch me!" I shouted back over my shoulder as I raced down the road. Before I knew it, I was slipping and falling onto my knees. Two sharp stalagmite icicles pierced through my right knee. The wounds were deep.

Mom kept me in bed for weeks but the wounds refused to heal. They became infected and I could barely walk. Dad was afraid I might lose my leg. Finally, in desperation, Mother went to a druggist in Tientsin. "Here, try this," he said. "It's called penicillin." It had just been formulated, but Mom was ready to try anything. She applied the brown paste to my wounds. Though it smelled terrible, I began to heal and was soon well and getting into more trouble. Consequently, I was one of the first trial users of antibiotics.

In the summertime we took trips to Paitaho Beach on the Pacific coast. There was a long expanse of sandy beach with pavilions to change in. Bathers would bring their teakettles and heat water on little stoves provided on the beach for the traditional four o'clock tea.

Often, our aunts and two cousins, Woogie and Dickie, would join us. Aunt Alice was married to a Scotsman named Robert Cameron but Carrie was still single. (Even though Dickie was a girl, they named her Dick because she was born between Tom and Harry.) Mom did a terrific breaststroke, and could swim to the jetty with me on her back.

It was while we were at the beach that Mother noticed the horizon black with ships steaming across the straits to China. "Look, Tom, those ships that are trailing black smoke behind them must be Japanese. I can see the red sun insignia on their smokestacks. Do you suppose they are coming to take over China's ports and invade China?"

"No, it would be ridiculous," Dad snorted. "Chiang Kai-shek, the leader of the Nationalist Party, has good control over the Chinese even though some of the factions are not unified. He also is getting support from Mao Tse-tung, a young, enthusiastic Communist who has trained a large army. Plus, we foreigners, now happily ensconced in China and doing a lot of trade with the Chinese, would never allow it. Surely they will put up a fight!"

By 1937, however, the Japanese had taken over Shanghai and then moved northward to Peking and Tientsin. The Japanese-Chinese war was on and the foreign countries stood by and did nothing about it.

"What is that thunder coming from the hills, Dad?" There was a constant rumble that rattled the windows and woke me up at night. It had been going on for days. "It's just the guerrillas," Dad replied with a shrug. "Go back to sleep."

"What are gorillas doing in China?" I thought. "And how can they make so much noise? They must be tearing down the mountains!"

Mao had broken away from the Nationalist Party and had marched his band of renegade Communists up to the mountains in the northeast. There they lived in caves while they practiced their heavy artillery and Mao trained them for his militia. His promise of a better land, where the people would be in charge of their own farms and factories while giving a certain amount of their profits to the state, seemed to make sense to the Chinese peasants. They had been exploited by warlords and emperors for such a long time. His band of guerrillas, which burgeoned as he marched through China, soon demolished the Nationalists and engaged the Japanese in warfare.

Harry stood with tousled hair and solemn brown eyes at the edge of the pond.

"You want me to climb the bank and get that red hollyhock on the other side of Dad's barbed wire fence?" His voice had an incredulous ring to it.

"Please, Harry, that double red one is a color I've never had before." One of the things we loved to do was squeeze the juice from the petals and paint pictures with the colorful dye. Sometimes we painted our faces and pretended we were Indians.

Reaching over the barbed wire fence that Dad had stretched along the inside wall to keep out robbers, Harry tried to grasp the desired flower. His foot slipped on the wet mud of the bank and a barb raked his arm, tearing a large piece of flesh out of it.

How guilty I felt as the servants, responding to Harry's calls for help, came rushing to the rescue. "I'm sorry, I'm sorry," I cried as the whole parade headed for the house. First came Harry with Dad supporting his arm in the air to slow down the bleeding; then Mom, followed by the amahs, and finally Da Nang and Boy, looking upset because he should be setting the table. Dad took Harry down the walks and straight to the library where the usual gentian violet treatment was given. I wonder today if he has ever forgiven me for the lifelong scar left on his forearm.

One other occurrence happened to Harry. "Hey, Sylvia, look at this ripe tomato I just got out of the garden," he shouted, brandishing the red fruit in the air. Dad had decided to take up falconry and had a beautiful but ferocious bird on his leather sleeve. When he took the hood off the bird, it surveyed the territory and spied Harry's red tomato. Before Dad could stop it, the falcon flew from its perch on his arm straight to the red tomato just as Harry was ready to take a bite. The falcon must have thought it was red meat and, sinking his talons into the tomato, he bombarded poor Harry in the face, knocking him down. To this day Harry has a fear of birds, even though he's out each morning lobstering with the seagulls.

We had several incidents that occurred with Dad's collection of livestock. One large gander had a dislike for Mom. Every time she tried to walk out in the gardens, he would sneak behind her and, with neck outstretched, run at her hissing and flapping his wings. "I hate that goose!" Mom would say as she ran into the house.

Another time, Tom was crouching down to shoot one of his agate marbles. The boys often played marbles, a game where you draw a circle on the ground, place all your marbles in the center and take turns trying to shoot your opponent's marbles out of the ring with one of yours. The one with the most marbles was the winner. Our big tom turkey spotted him and, thinking he was an adversary, jumped on his back with wings outstretched, flapping and pecking the back of his neck. Luckily one of the gardeners was close by and saved him, because Harry and I just stood frozen with our mouths open. Now Tom has a terrific respect for turkeys, even though they are named after him.

CHAPTER 6
CHINESE CUSTOMS

Although it was taboo to venture out of the iron gates, my curiosity got the best of me one morning and I wandered outside. In a field of millet I came across a tiny baby. Although it lay dressed in padded clothing, with nails and hair polished and combed as if it was going to a party, it was dead. On her (I believe it was a baby girl) forehead was a round, red spot and in the blanket, wrapped perfectly around her chubby body, were small trinkets and Chinese toys. With Dresden face she lay in calm repose. I was shocked!

No parents were around as far as I could determine, so, completely perplexed, I pushed back the row of millet and ran back to the house.

"The Chinese have strange customs, dear." Mother was sitting on a wicker chair on the terrace when I questioned her. Pulling me onto her lap, she explained, "They worship their ancestors believing that the older you are, the more knowledge you have obtained and therefore the more valuable you become. The grandparents are kept fed but the baby had to be discarded when they found they couldn't feed everyone. It was probably given as an offering to the Chinese gods." We have plenty of food, I thought to myself; I would have liked to have kept that baby.

The lack of value the Chinese attributed to life was further impressed upon me in 1989 when the Communist leaders killed their educated young college students just because they were demonstrating. On June 12th, the army with tanks came into Tiananmen Square and started to shoot into the crowd. The supporters of the democracy movement, rallying behind a statue they had made of the Goddess of Democracy, were protesting against Communism. One young boy actually stood before a tank and was crushed. The general secretary of the Communist party, Zhao Ziyang, a reformer who didn't believe in Mao's doctrines, tried to help the students and encouraged them. Of the 10,000 college students, about 1,000 were killed. *Newsweek* described it as "a horrible bloodbath." What a loss it was of good young minds. Officials deemed sympathetic to the protests were demoted or purged, and the Communist Government will not allow any references to the incident now.

"May I go, really?" I didn't get a chance to see Tientsin often, so I was really excited. The only other Chinese I had contact with besides the servants was the popsicle man who came, selling his frozen, flavored ice on a stick at the back fence of our garden.

"If you behave and hold Amah's hand," Mother said as she dressed me. Number Two Amah did the shopping for Da Nang each week. She would go into town in a rickshaw, and I was thrilled that Mother trusted me to go with her.

The Chinese shopping area of Tientsin was an enigma. Plucked chickens and shiny brown Peking ducks were trussed and hung from rafters, while glazed-eyed fish lay lined up on pallets. Litchi nuts and bamboo shoots filled straw baskets on the ground. Chinese cabbage, corn, turnips, sweet potatoes, and leeks made colorful pyramids on the tables. The pungent odor of spices mixed with cigarette smoke, incense, and fish almost made me choke, but I held tightly to Amah's hand as she bargained her way along the row of concessions.

One of the booths had kites, lanterns, and skewers of bright red lady apples. The small apples were threaded, six at a time, and dipped in a hard sugar coating. "I want one, Amah!" I demanded, pointing at the bright, spired display.

The deep, leathery creases of her face relaxed into a knowing smile as she reached deeply into her baggy black pants and produced a ragged drawstring money purse. Dad did not allot the servants much money, so she had to count the yen with care to make sure she had enough. Triumphantly, I marched off crunching through the hard surface of the tart apples while juice and sugar covered my face.

While we were at the market, I noticed a couple of well-dressed Chinese ladies sitting on a bench. Their feet were about four inches long and were covered with embroidered satin shoes. They looked like the shoes

I would put on my doll. I pointed it out to Amah, but she only nodded her head and pulled me away.

Later, I mentioned it to Dad and his explanation was that an emperor during the Han dynasty made all the children of his province bind their feet as soon as they were born because his daughter had small feet. (Chinese also believed that people with big ears were very intelligent because Confucius had big ears.) To me, footbinding, which is done when a little girl is only a few months old, resembles the body piercing which we see so much today. However, the difference is that the person today is usually old enough to make such a decision on their own.

When the child's foot was bound, it was twisted so that the toes were bent down to touch the heel of the foot. Strong linen bindings were bandaged tightly to hold the foot in this position and the bound feet were powdered and perfumed to keep down the odor.

In *The Body as Attire: Shifting Meanings of Footbinding in Seventeenth Century China*, Dorothy Ko points out, "It was neither a uniform practice across regions, nor did it sustain a timeless core of meanings." Footbinding became the norm for elite Han Chinese females during the Ming dynasty. Ko felt that footbinding had a high cultural prestige connected with it. Therefore the hairstyles, clothing, and foot coverings were standard criteria for evaluating the people. Residents of Yunnan province were presented as close kin to the Han Chinese because their women had bound feet, too. They felt that it set them apart from the barbarians who often bared their feet.

Ko related a story about one of the barbarian tribes raiding a village and capturing some of the Han women for their concubines. Having no way to transport them, they made them run behind their mounts. The foot-bound women, barely able to hobble, were unable to keep up, so the barbarians cut off their feet and they bled to death.

This sounds too dumb and brutal to be completely true. Perhaps they unbound the poor ladies' feet, found that the toes were permanently bent under, and tried to cut them off. Otherwise, why would someone dismember something they considered their "spoils of war"?

In the sixteenth century, the foot-bound woman marked the cultural lines between "us" and "them." She represented the boundaries of Chinese "national" identity before the age of modern nationalism. In the seventeenth century, it was considered female attire, like the gold hoops some wear through their noses, ears, and navels today.

Some think that the small, highly decorated foot was appealing to Chinese men or at least gave them a feeling of dominance over a woman who was barely able to walk. Consequently, it continued in different provinces until the 1900s, when the teaching of missionaries and health workers put a stop to most of it. When I think of Mother's problems and pain with her deformed foot, I cannot see how people allowed this to go on for so long.

Another cultural custom of the Chinese was to celebrate the New Year, usually in February, according to the position of the full moon. All Chinese people celebrated the event no matter how young or old, in contrast to our country, where there are different holidays with the variety of religions.

The Chinese New Year always began with fireworks in the streets. Children held sparklers and strings of crackers that would go off with a bang, bang, bang! The big parades through the streets would follow in the evening with huge dragons carried through the streets by six to ten men. Of course there would be lots of banners and Chinese music and gay, colorful lanterns. As the parade ended, fireworks would light up the sky until late in the evening. It was the one time all year that the Chinese really let it all hang out.

What stays in my memory most was the custom of leaving a small coin for good luck under the children's pillow. Mother would tiptoe into our room that night and tuck a little red paper packet under our pillow with Chinese money in it to signify happiness and prosperity.

CHAPTER 7
BEGINNING OF WORLD WAR II

On the other side of the Pacific, a dictator was starting his rise to power. After the defeat of Germany in World War I, Adolf Hitler, an Austrian soldier from the Bavarian army in France, attended a meeting of the German Workers' Party, where his views against the Jews and Socialists were quickly accepted. He was blaming these groups for the country's lack of patriotism, will to fight, and poverty. He also advocated a "super" race that would exclude Jews and other ethnic groups. Enormous crowds listened to his agitated speeches and were soon cheering him on, with right arm extended, shouting, "Heil, Hitler!"

Coming to power in 1933, Hitler started barring Jews from shops, civil service jobs, and universities. By 1942, Czechoslovakia, which had been taken over by Germany in 1938, was ordered to strip Jews of their identity and exterminate them. They were put into concentration camps, where they were used as human guinea pigs, gassed in showers, or starved to death. Their bodies were then either bulldozed into shallow pits or cremated in ovens such as those found in Auschwitz.

Besides the millions of Jews that were eradicated, Gypsies, handicapped people, homosexuals, communists, and even some of the Soviet soldiers Hitler captured were killed. It wasn't until Hitler sent his armies against Poland that Britain and France joined in the war, but by 1940 he still conquered Poland and went on to ravage Denmark, Norway, Belgium, and the Netherlands. The United States joined in to help their allies, but not until the storming of Normandy did the British and American troops finally defeat the Germans. World War II ended in 1945 and Hitler committed suicide on April 30, 1945. The last German soldier surrendered on May 7, 1945.

Every night after supper, my dad would go to his study and glue his ear to the Phillips radio. He was concerned that the United States would enter the war and help the British. Edward R. Murrow would broadcast the German atrocities from the BBC in London, trying to tell of the hardships of the English people, but President Roosevelt was reluctant to get involved.

Chapter 8
CAPTURED

The Japanese meanwhile were getting increasingly aggressive. Entering across the Bering Strait, they had already taken over one of the small towns in Alaska.

Dad had a premonition that things were going to get ugly. The Tientsin newspaper reported one morning that the British had to barricade their concession due to the escalation of the Japanese invasion. Dad rounded up Mom's jewelry, some of his bonds, and his Phillips radio. Pacing off several yards behind the house, he got one of the gardeners to dig a big hole in the ground and bury the lot.

On December 8, 1941 (actually December 7 in America), a clanging on the wrought iron gate disturbed our tranquil lunch, or "tiffin," as the British call it. It was noon and we had just started eating.

"Let them in," Dad told the gardener. He knew who it was. That morning, it had been announced that the city of Tientsin was surrounded by the Japanese.

Six lavishly embellished Japanese officers came down the path and marched up to the front door. Standing three abreast, they banged at the door, demanding to see the owner of the house.

With eyes like slits and jowls bulging over their tight braided collars, they sneered at Dad. I noticed their ruddy countenances, possibly from drinking too much saké the night before. In khaki uniforms with tiers of gold braid and rows of medals, each carried a Samurai sword and pistol at his side.

"We have just bombed your Pearl Harbor this morning," one officer announced. "You are now prisoners of war!"

With trepidation, I peeked around Boy's white cotton trousers. Fear, but also excitement, gripped me. What were they going to do with us and would Dad order them away?

Dad did not resist, however, and Mother was told she had to pack in seven minutes. She packed what she could, mainly clothes and pictures. None of the silver, cut glass, and antiques was disturbed. All was left behind. Dad rushed about the house, closing up and giving instructions to the servants. The livestock and dogs had to be fed and the gardens tended to. Most of the servants left, but the gardener stayed on. "Don't worry," Dad said, "we know America, our country, is so strong it will soon squash these little yellow devils." To the boys and me he said, "We'll be back home soon, just do as they say so no one will get hurt." Little did we know that the items packed in our steamer trunks were all we would have for the next three and a half years, and that we were leaving our beautiful home, never to return. My porcelain doll sat on the hollyhock bedspread in our bedroom for four years. After the war, Aunt Alice went back to the house and sent Mother some of her cut glass and my poor ragged doll.

An old Baptist parsonage was selected by the Japanese for our temporary residence, and though we were not free to move about, Dad was given a special pass to take care of his affairs and work. After the flood, Dunlop closed and, on January 5, 1940, Dad started working for the COMIL Oil Company. The company handled such things as peanut and sesame oil, not crude oil. For a long time I thought he was in the crude oil business.

Around the English concession, the Japanese had put up barbed wire barricades that were patrolled by Japanese soldiers. The parsonage, at 10 Downing Street, had a balconied servants' quarters behind a brick building. We were put in these three small rooms on the second floor, accessible only by the balcony. At the end was a small cold bathroom. It was quite an experience making my way at night to the freezing, pull-chain toilet at the end of the balcony. My derrière remembers it well.

There was a small walled-in courtyard around the parsonage, and in this "prison" I became very bored. My favorite pastime was peering out at the peddlers and rickshaws through the large cast-iron gate. One day, to the delight of a passing "bing" peddler, I had exchanged a broken shoelace for a bright, pink piece of hemp. He stopped, with his bamboo shoulder pole that held a blackened cooking pot suspended from one end, and the dough, chopped leeks, and peanut oil in a sack suspended from the other. Laughing with glee, he slapped his sides, showing his nicotine-stained teeth. The Chinese have always enjoyed jokes and often find miniscule quirks in life comical.

It was during this time that Dad started teaching me algebra. He had found a blackboard and lavishly covered it with algebraic equations. "This equals to that and that gives you this," he would say, and then erasing the board with a flourish, he would beam at me like I got it. Only I didn't get it, and the tears would start to flow like the Yangtze River. I was only eight years old and was very confused about something he seemed to think so simple. Plus, I wanted badly to please him.

"If you cry one more time, I'll give you a caning," Dad said with annoyance. He tried explaining again, covering the board with equations, but my mind went dead and all I could do was sob while tears ran down my cheeks. Off I was marched to the other room where Dad procured a short bamboo stick. "Hold out your hands," he demanded. Whack! Whack! Whack! Each hand got six licks. It was the worst pain I had endured in my short life.

After that, I avoided my father as much as I could. The swelling eventually went down in my hands and I could close them again, but it never cured me of crying. Luckily, he gave up the idea of teaching me. Instead, he started me in school for the first time. Girls were not supposed to attend school in China, but the British had set up a small co-ed school in the city. It was funny, because the first thing they taught was that there were six letters in my first name, quite a far cry from the long equations in algebra.

By February 1942, we were moved to Singapore Road. It was clear that the Japanese didn't know what to do with us as they were concentrating on the war in the Pacific. They had captured Indonesia and the islands of Malaysia, where they got supplies of rubber for their war machinery. Australia was the next country they would invade. Thank goodness, they were stopped by our troops before they got a foothold and the Aussies have never forgotten it.

The Germans were also becoming more and more powerful, gobbling up most of the countries of Europe except for England, Spain, Switzerland, and Italy. In the *Richmond Times-Dispatch*, a February 1991 article recounts the sighting of German U-boats off the coast of Virginia and North Carolina and the torpedoing of merchant vessels along the Atlantic coast from Canada to Florida. This was the first contact with the war that the American coast felt. The military commanders refused to report it and asked the people of North Carolina to keep it a secret.

After 400 ships were destroyed, the military sent out U.S. airplanes to drop depth charges and Army bombers that attacked and finally dispersed the U-boats; Germany didn't send over any more. The Navy kept this all a secret, which makes one wonder what sort of secrets are being hidden from us today as we face the problems with terrorists and the Middle East wars.

Meanwhile, Dad sent Boy to the Willows on his bicycle to obtain some more clothing and important papers. Boy had to sneak through the Japanese barricade and pretend he was delivering supplies to the soldiers. On his way back, Boy was searched, but they accepted his fabricated story.

"I've contacted the Swiss agency in hopes to get us passports to leave the country," Dad informed us. So on September 1, we all had pictures taken at the embassy and received passports, but the last ship that could take us was full and we were left at the mercy of the Japs. However, we were children and the danger of the situation didn't have an impact on us at this time.

"Let me join, please!" The boys and I were bored being confined in the English concession, so Tom decided he would start a secret club. They only wanted their friends, since their aim was to shoot at bullies around the concession with their slingshots.

"Okay," Tom said, "only you have to make our ammunition."

In the middle of the town was an immense mound of bricks with a hole in the center. Into this "fort" I climbed and spent afternoons rolling mud into balls that I dried on the shelves of bricks jutting out in the interior walls.

The club dispersed, however, when Tom (who was beginning to notice girls) got interested in a little blonde who lived in the apartment house across from our fort.

"I bet I can hit her window with my slingshot and get her to look out," he said.

Carefully aiming his trusty slingshot, with one of my biggest mud balls in it, he fired away. To his dismay, there was a tinkling of broken glass and, instead of the cute little girl, an irate father leaned out of the broken window shaking his fist at us and yelling for the police. You never saw three kids climb out of a brick pile and run for home so fast!

One Leaf in Time

The Christmas of 1942, Dad gave me a little autograph book, and Tom and Harry were the first to write in it. Tom wrote: "I thought and thought and thought in vain. At last I thought I'd sign my name." And Harry wrote: "First comes love, then comes marriage, then comes Sylvia with a baby carriage." They both signed their names.

This book became very precious to me, as many of my camp friends signed it during our camp years. I treasure the signatures of nuns, bishops, and brothers who kept us going when we became depressed and hopeless, and also the signature of my ship companion, signed with a flourish across a page, though our lives never crossed paths again.

By March, the Japanese had decided they had a place to keep us. Dad was alerted and resigned his position at COMIL. Chung Mei, his partner, took over the carpet factory they had started.

Again, the bayonet-toting Japanese soldiers came to the gates. "You come with us. Pack one suitcase—go on train," they said, as they dragged us out into the street. Number One Amah was with us and, as we staggered out of the parsonage, she interposed her body between us. Defying the drawn bayonets, she held us behind her and declared, "You will have to kill me first before you take these children!" Of course she spoke in Cantonese, but the gesture was enough. One of the soldiers pointed his gun at Amah's forehead and was ready to shoot, but the feisty little woman stood firm. Dad, who could speak seven dialects of Chinese fluently, ordered her to step aside and she reluctantly obeyed him. It was a tense moment; I could feel my heart pounding. How horrible to think of Amah murdered!

We quickly got our belongings together and lined up, escorted by the Japanese. Each of us carried a large trunk or suitcase with all we could jam into it. Not knowing where we were to be taken, we concentrated on warm clothing and blankets.

Belgians, Dutch, French, British, Russians, and Americans, all dragging their suitcases, marched single file to the train station on the other side of town. As we were trudging along through the streets lined with sympathetic Chinese, Number Two Amah stepped out of the crowd with a small cotton bag and tucked it into Tom's hand. "Take," was all she said. It contained all her life savings. He tried to give it back, but she disappeared into the crowd.

We were a motley crew, people of all ages, occupations, religions, and nationalities, carrying or wearing whatever we felt dear. The White

Russian ladies, part of the group that had opposed the Bolsheviks decades earlier, had on their mink stoles and jewelry, the children carried favorite toys or food. The Salvation Army members carried their instruments, and the nuns, brothers, and missionaries, dressed in habit, carried their bibles. One Salvation Army member had a tuba that kept getting in everyone's way, but he was so robust and jolly, nobody minded.

The atmosphere was definitely solemn. Sweating as we carried our heavy burdens, we labored up the hill to the train station (the same station Mother had come into about twelve years before.) Without any explanation as to our destination, the Japanese loaded us into the cars with great haste. There must have been at least five hundred men, women, and children.

Dad made sure we stayed together and didn't get separated because he wasn't certain the train would stop at only one destination. It had broken his heart to have to plait my long hair and chop it off earlier. If we were separated, my long hair would be difficult to manage, so I got my first real haircut.

Japanese changing flag to "Rising Sun" in takeover of Tientsin, 1937

My father, Thomas Churchill

My mother, Ethel Lightfoot Churchill

Mom, Dad, Tommy, and me on a brick-and-cinder fountain wall

Grape arbor bare after the flood—
Tom, me, and Harry

They tried to gussy me up, but I was always
a tomboy.

St. Joseph's School for Boys

Harry in "white jacket" with his class

Dad, Tom, Woogie, and Aunt Carrie at the beach

Harry, Mom, Tom, and me in the waters at Paitaho Beach

Sledding on the Grand Canal with Dad and Aunt Carrie

Me, age 7

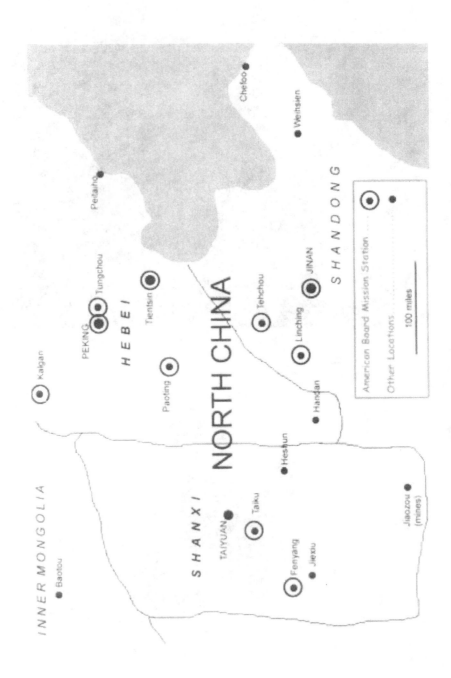

CHAPTER 9
WEIHSIEN COMPOUND

"Click, clack, chunk; click, clack, chunk," whoosh! We were jammed like sardines in the passenger car of the train. There wasn't enough space to sit with the luggage, so Dad pushed the trunks between facing seats and had us lie over them. Mom sat at the end of the seat and held my head in her lap.

Where were we going? How would they treat us? The papers were already informing us of the atrocities that the Germans were inflicting on their prisoners in Germany.

One paper reported that a German soldier had smashed a little boy's head against a cement wall in a train station because the child refused to give up his apple. There were horrible pictures of the boy's brains and blood spattered on the wall.

Although night had fallen, and we were all sleepy, I listened to the men huddled together discussing the situation and how to handle it best. The Marines stationed in Northern China, numbering somewhere around 200, had been captured by the Japanese and were put into concentration camps also, but they were still convinced that the United States and Britain would soon come to our aid and punish the Japanese for their impudence. There was a rumor that we were traveling inland to Shantung province.

What we did not know was that close to 125,000 civilians—men, women, and children—were being incarcerated in prisons around China. The Japanese called them "containment camps." Some were at Hong Kong, others around Shanghai, and others up the river from Shanghai. Some internees were marched through the lower provinces of China, and others were put into cattle trains and sent to Manchuria.

It was dawn when we arrived. "Blimey, don't push. We'll see these yellow devils soon enough." A British teacher with black cropped hair was helping the women and children climb into open logging trucks, again lugging their various pieces of baggage with them. We bumped along a dusty road to the town of Weihsien and then to the camp a few miles on the outskirts of town.

Near noon the inhabitants of the town turned out en masse to watch the proceedings. They jeered at the Japanese and sometimes at us, not siding with one or the other but trying to get their licks in without aggravating the Japs enough to be shot. Some were spitting and shaking their fists while keeping a safe distance in case the tiger turned.

"Look at all the food set out on mats and covered with flies," said Mom. A small town with no industry, Weihsien had to rely mostly on its farming. We drove through the medieval-size gates and out into the country, where the Japanese had taken over a Presbyterian missionary college that had been the sole support of the town, in which to contain us. It was called Courtyard of the Happy Way.

At the sight of the six-sided, gray brick compound with turrets on each corner, for the first time, I was numbed by fear. From each turret projected a machine gun aimed directly at us, and along the walls were thick rows of electrified barbed wire with more electrified wires on top. The whole compound, which was about three football fields wide and one deep, looked grim. Huge metal gates slammed behind us as we drove in. "Mother," I whispered, as I clung to her hand, "I'm scared." Even Tom and Harry, who were usually quite daring, looked pale and were biting their lips.

With bayonets drawn, uniformed guards jostled us into a large dirt playing field. They were shouting commands in Japanese, which we did not understand, but it didn't take a genius to understand the gestures and those sharp, pointed bayonets. Finally they sorted us into family groups and lined us up in long rows. As they paced back and forth in front of us, we got our first introduction to the men who would be our jailers for the next three years.

They were a raggle-taggle bunch, mostly rejects from the regular army due to physical ailments or high status of their kin in Japan. Some of the higher echelon could speak a little English, although it was short and stunted. Anyhow, they got it across that we would be housed in single rooms that were connected into rows or blocks. The single people were to occupy two large dormitories, one for men and one for the women, with about thirty-six square feet available to each person. This only gave them enough space for a bed and a trunk.

One Leaf in Time

In the blocks we were given one room to every four people, but as luck would have it, our family of five was assigned two rooms. With a view of one of the dormitories, we were flanked on one side by a robust Dutch family that had eleven members and a Belgian family on the other with a family of four. The Dutch family had only two rooms and the Belgians one, which caused a little animosity at first, but they soon got over it.

The camp was commanded by a general that we instantly disliked. Carrying a long sword that reached to the ground, he strode along our disheveled rows, passing out armbands. The armbands were made of muslin and were printed with our names in English and Japanese, our block number and age. (Mother embroidered ours later.) We were to wear them at all times and would be in serious trouble if caught without them.

With another Jap to translate, the general then gave us orders to organize our camp, selecting people to head up the food distribution, housing, sanitation, and medical needs. (We added the education and entertainment ourselves later.) A gentleman from the British-American Tobacco Company was put in charge, and he formed a town council. The purpose of this was to look into problems, referee any grievances, and see that the camp work was evenly distributed.

The internees, numbering about 3,000 at first, came not only from Tientsin, but Peking, Shanghai, and Tsingtao as well. Some of the brothers and sisters came from Chowtsun, located in Shantung Province. In an atmosphere of "none better than the rest," we were free from coveting thy neighbor's house or car or from the hassle of class status. Bankers, businessmen, doctors, lawyers, clergy, and teachers (all we needed was an Indian chief)—all were put in the same cauldron and had to make the best of it.

There were some grumbles about living spaces, but, though most of us were total strangers, we started living harmoniously together. Mother told me that when the chores were assigned, the ladies had to take turns cleaning the latrines. They were called water closets. I believe there were four and each had a big WC painted on the side of the cement building. Inside there were two long planks about a foot apart and underneath a long furrow filled with ashes. "You have to put your feet on each plank and squat over the hole. Only don't fall in," Mother cautioned me. It was not an easy task without a seat or handle to support you. Rather breezy, too, I recall.

The White Russian ladies put up a fuss when they were told they had to take their turn cleaning off the planks and scooping the refuse from the ashes to throw into an open sewer nearby. Finally, the town council stepped in and they did their smelly job grudgingly.

Every morning and night, we had to stand in front of our row of rooms to be counted. However, the Japs had trouble counting past ten, so the Dutch family of eleven always put them in a tizzy. They would go up the line scratching their heads counting and recounting, then stand and argue with each other. This was amusing enough, but quite to our surprise, Mrs. Bejongh produced another little Bejongh shortly after we arrived. (Mrs. Bejongh was a big, plump, jolly woman; we never even knew she was pregnant.) Now they had a count of twelve!

One morning, when baby Paul was crawling, Mrs. Bejongh decided to potty train him, so she left him inside on his little pot. It really puzzled the Japs as they counted and recounted the Bejongh family. They soon became nasty, spitting out threatening words to Mr. Bejongh. With a sigh and a shrug of her shoulders, Mrs. Bejongh disappeared into their rooms and came back proudly with little blond-haired Paul still sitting on his pot. Carrying him to the end of the row, she set him down in his place next to his sister. All but the Japanese had a wonderful laugh.

In one of our little rooms, Dad built himself a collapsible bed. He could lift it out of the way against the wall during the day and we had that space to sit and eat in. The second room had a bunk bed, which Harry and I slept in, and two cots that Tom and Mother occupied. The nine-by-twelve-foot space was so jammed with beds that there was only enough room to squeeze between. Each room had a small screened window almost to the ceiling. By the door, in the front, stood an old dilapidated coal stove. We looked at the whitewashed walls with holes smashed in them in dismay. The moldy ceiling and bare light bulb were such a change from our lovely home on Race Course Road.

Well, as soon as the weather got colder, Dad started to worry about us freezing without heat. As the stove had no stovepipes to exhaust the smoke, he had to find a supply of them. We had been told that there was a pile of coal at the back of the camp that we could dig for ourselves, so that was no problem.

He soon located the stockpile of stovepipes in the basement of the bachelor's dormitory. It was located close to block 22, where we were housed, and several big elm trees shaded it. On inquiry, Dad found that they were not to be given out to the prisoners but were saved for the Japanese quarters. Waiting until there was a moonless night, he blackened the boys' and his faces with soot, slipped out in the cover of the trees, and crept to the building. The guards had warned us that anyone found out of their rooms at night would be instantly shot, so it was terribly dangerous. Of course the boys thought of it as a wonderful "James Bond" adventure, but Dad knew the guards patrolled the grounds regularly and they would have to be careful.

As the boys were slim, Dad could lower them through a basement window and, while he stood watch, the boys passed up the pipes one by one. "I'll whistle 'The Whistler and His Dog' as a signal if a guard approaches," Dad told the boys. This was a tune that has no words to it, but was very familiar to the boys. Luckily, no guards came by and the boys accomplished their task without incident. Stovepipes were installed, not only on our stove, but on several neighbors' stoves as well.

When they handed out jobs, Dad was put to work as the baker. Three large clay ovens were located in buildings near the playing field. Mixing the wormy flour and stoking the fires with coal kept him busy most of the day. He often came back drenched in perspiration and terribly tired, but he never lost his sense of humor.

When we had to use the toilet at night (especially the children), we used chamber pots. During the day, they were emptied into open sewers in the compound. Our Belgian neighbor, who had been president of the largest bank in China, was dead meat for Dad. Mr. Pandre would cover his chamber pot with a delicate French doily and perform his task with the air of an English butler. Dad would call out from our doorway, "Hey, Pandre, you going for seconds?" then laugh himself silly as Mr. Pandre's face turned red. After a few weeks the lace doily disappeared and Mr. Pandre, brandishing the pot, would jovially return a few remarks. Once he said, "I'll get you some too if you want."

Serving the meals was Mom's job. Queues of internees, sometimes 1,000, would snake out the door of the flimsy log dining hall. Mom had to stand with a few other women, ladling out stew or soup for hours. It was hard on her, especially with her deformed leg, but she never complained and, for a bonus, she could sometimes bring home leftovers.

Food was not scarce at first, but it was far from substantial. We did get turnips, cabbage, and sweet potatoes that were brought in by neighboring farmers. Meat was kept on trucks for days without refrigeration and often had maggots in it. The soup was seasoned with Chinese leeks, but there were no spices. If it hadn't been for sweet potatoes, we would have been sadly deficient in Vitamins A and C because there was no milk, fruit, or juices. Instead, we drank soybean tea. It was my duty to get a small pail of soybean tea, walking the twenty blocks back to our rooms. With no sugar or cream, it was quite distasteful at first. Now nutritionists are proclaiming the benefits of soy. So, go figure!

As far as meat, Langdon Gilkey, a fellow internee who went on to write a book about his experiences in the camp, claims we had an occasional hamburger. I don't recall them, and Gilkey may have had special treatment because he was the cook. There was some sinewy horse meat at times in stew, but it had gray veins and gristle and was on the verge of being spoiled due to lack of refrigeration.

Nothing was wasted. All unused bread was soaked overnight in big vats with a little shredded orange peel (the only touch of citrus that we had in our diet). It was heated in the morning as our porridge and served with soybean tea. The Chinese peasants hated the Japanese and tried to send us all they could, but they were starving themselves and under strict surveillance by the Japs.

Winters were quite severe in Weihsien. With our clothes getting threadbare by the second year, Mother kept busy pulling out her sewing basket. Layering the clothes we had and passing down sweaters and socks helped a little. "Sylvia, I need some water for washing," Mom would say, and off I would go with my little bucket—the same one that I used to carry tea back from the dining hall to our rooms. Sometimes the pump handle would be frozen and I had to break away the ice and melt snow to prime it. With all my strength, pump handle in both hands, I would jump up and come down with full force . . . No water. Collecting myself and blowing on my frozen hands, I'd try it again until, with a squish, the pump cooperated. Then I'd take the bucket of water back to our room to be heated on the pot-bellied stove.

Though it was cold, like all children, we ventured out into the snow, throwing snowballs at each other with our bare hands. We had quite a few snowfalls, as the climate was very much like New England. Sometimes,

Dad had to let the stove burn out, as we were getting low on coal. We'd sit, teeth chattering, in our beds, while Mother dried out our clothes on a line over the stove. Those were the bad days, as the thought of being prisoners and subject to death at any time weighed heavy on our minds. Dad tried to keep us busy and Mother taught me to knit and sew, but we still felt depressed.

Winston Churchill once said, "We make a living by what we get. We make a life by what we give." Several of the internees made an example of this.

One of the most colorful of these was a Trappist monk. His name was Father Martin. In his sect he was sworn to a life of fasting and silence. He was not even supposed to mingle with others. Dragged from his monastery and thrown in with a huge group of people should have been desolating; instead, Father Martin turned out to be the most social person in camp. With his twinkling blue eyes and constant good humor he would visit the widows and single young women, dressed in a well-pressed white linen suit, and join them for dinner, sometimes sharing a bottle of Chinese whiskey with them. Everyone knew and loved him. With his jaunty Panama hat perched over a bushy, black beard and curly long hair, he was often seen chatting with people in the compound.

What we were not aware of was that he had started a black market over the wall with the Chinese! During the internment, he often donned his heavy robes and prayed for hours under the camp walls. He looked so pious in his homespun Woolsey frock that even the Japanese sentries would cross themselves as they passed by. We did not realize what was going on until we found eggs, whiskey, and extra veggies being passed out to the people that were suffering most from the lack of food or sickness.

The good father was somehow corresponding with the Chinese farmers as they brought in our days' rations or had found a hole in the wall that he could whisper through. Then, at the appointed time, he would send money in a small basket over the wall and the farmer would send the basket back with eggs in it. Not only was this dangerous because of the electrified wire along the top of the wall, but guards frequently made their rounds patrolling the city-block-sized compound. When the basket of eggs was passed over the wall, Father Martin would hurriedly place the eggs under his robes, kneeling fervently in prayer until the guard was gone.

Soon the black market idea caught on and others joined in to provide food and whiskey to our tables. (The Chinese were quite adept at making whiskey from all the corn that was grown in this area.)

Sadly enough, one day Father Martin was caught in the act. The Japanese soldiers bound his hands and marched him off to a jail tower for a month. We were all afraid that he would suffer worse consequences and breathed a sigh of relief that he was not tortured or killed. The irony of it all was that he was given the solitary confinement he had chosen for his lifestyle anyway, as a Trappist monk is supposed to speak to no one and spend his life in confinement and prayer.

We all rejoiced. His lady friends brought cookies and notes and threw them through the bars into his cell. They even made up words put to the tune of "If I Had the Wings of an Angel." Everyone around camp was singing it:

> Oh, meet me tonight in the moonlight,
> Oh, meet me there all alone.
> For I have a sad story to tell you,
> A story that's never been known.
> Oh, they trapped me a Trappist last Wednesday,
> Now few are the eggs to be fried.
> Alone in a dark cell I ponder
> If my clients are hollow inside.
> For here there is no one to buy from,
> No one to help me along.
> I'm missing the bustle of business
> Away from the hungering throng.
> For there is a big bag on the outside
> Overflowing with honey and jam,
> But how can I get it to this side
> Till the bootleggers know where I am.
> Many thanks to my friends; your good wishes
> Flooded my lonely cell yesterday.
> Oh, why can't I swim like the fishes?
> So the rain might have washed me away.
> But confinement has some compensation,
> I'm not in a rush to be free;

One Leaf in Time

Before it was Tsingtao that fed me,
Now my food comes from dining room three.
I hope that the time passes swiftly
And I will be seeing you soon.
Then you'll find me right back in harness,
By the light of the silvery moon.

I'm not sure whether Father Martin or one of his admirers wrote this, but it caught on and became very popular.

The poor farmer who was supplying the eggs was not so fortunate. He was captured, tortured, and hung outside the wall for three days until he was finally shot. We had to listen to his screams as he was being tortured and the wailing of his family after he died. "That poor man," I cried. "He was only trying to make some money for his family." Mother tried to console me, but I couldn't forget the sound and the thoughts of that poor Chinaman dangling from the barbed wire. It was terribly frightening and reminded us that our captors were not to be taken for granted.

Another incident that occurred in the camp involved one of the White Russian women, a woman named Mrs. Chevasky. She was quite a troublemaker anyway. (She was one of the women who had refused to clean the latrines when it was their turn.) The sewers were getting filled to the brim, permeating the camp with an awful odor and collecting hoards of flies. Actually it was the town council's job to do something about it, but this dumpy, red-haired, boisterous bastion of a lady took it into her own hands.

Confronting the Japanese general, whom we all hated, in the area between our block and the dormitory building, she blocked his path. (We had nicknamed him "Gesundheit," because he frequently snarled a Japanese word that sounded very similar.) We all stood agape as she sputtered on. Shaking a finger in Gesundheit's face, she threatened to notify the Russian embassy about the unsanitary conditions. What was this woman thinking? General Gesundheit stepped back with a cold stare on his frozen face, eyes squinted into slits and mouth barely visible over a greasy chin. Without uttering a word, he unsheathed the samurai sword that hung from his barrel-like body and with a swift upward sweep, slashed it across the woman's face. Mrs. Chevasky let out a piercing scream as the large wound gapped open, spewing blood and tissue over her.

I don't remember what happened after that, but we never saw that woman again. She was either too embarrassed to show her scarred face or she may have died from infection, but General Gesundheit still strutted about the camp like a pompous peacock.

After that, we did have the sewers emptied. Two Chinese coolies came in each month with a big basket that they carried between them on a pole. They were ragged and filthy, but these men later became our source of information for the events and progress of the war. They evidently hid thin rice paper up their noses when they entered the camp and, typical of the Chinese coolie, would blow their noses robustly into the dust as they passed by one of the camp leaders. On the paper, they could only print small scraps of information, but it gave us a boost to know that the battle was being won by the British and Americans. Of course, they were constantly in danger of being caught, having to wait until the Japanese guard turned his back. The contents of our sewers were then spread over the fields to fertilize the crops that eventually fed us. Talk about recycling!

Through them, we learned how the Japanese had lost the Battle of the Coral Sea and were defeated on the small island of Midway, which ended their expansion into the eastern part of the Pacific. By March 1943, they were forced to retreat across the Yangtze and, by March 1944, crossed over the border of India. In June, the U.S. sent B-29 Superfortresses over Japan, strafing and bombing the main cities. After many bloody battles at Saipan, Guam, the Philippines, and Leyte Island, the U.S. Pacific Fleet defeated the Japanese fleet in the Battle of Leyte Gulf. By January 1945, the Allies had reopened a land route to China and, with terrible loss of life, took over Iwo Jima and Okinawa Island, forcing the Japanese to surrender in China. Of course we did not hear of all this until we were liberated, but the scraps of information that we received from these "spies" helped to buoy up our spirits. Many of the men were even planning to take over the camp.

A famous figure who gave so much of himself was Eric Liddell. This Scottish hero, after winning a gold medal in the Olympics, turned to missionary work in China. When the Japanese were torturing two Chinese leaders in a town, Eric slipped in during the night with an ox cart and saved both men, though one had been wounded severely and the other had his throat slit. Sneaking into the Japanese camp in the dark, he bundled the men up and carried them over his back, covering them up with hay in the cart.

Working with the children in the camp, he encouraged sports and set up a "spring Olympics," in which we all competed. I remember running around the inside walls of the camp and getting terribly out of breath. Other games were the shot put, high jumps, and soccer. Tom recalls Eric teaching the boys rounders, tennis, and basketball. After twenty years in China, this brave Scotsman succumbed to a brain tumor and died at the age of forty-three, six months before we were liberated.

Had this man not uplifted our spirits with his enthusiasm and love of sports, many of the internees would not have been able to cope with the restricted and fearful circumstances we were put into. The Bible says, "As much as you do for your fellow man, you are doing for me." Eric Liddell lived this philosophy during his short life.

Also lifting the morale and buoying us up through religion were the Catholic monks, brothers, and sisters. They visited the sick, set up a hospital in one of the vacant buildings, and gathered us together in an open field to sing the old familiar songs of the day.

Imagine at least three hundred people singing "It's a Long Way to Tipperary," "My Old Kentucky Home," "When Irish Eyes Are Smiling," and "Little Brown Jug"—"tip me up and down she goes!" "Smile the While You Bid Me Fond Adieu" was one of my favorites. We would hold hands and sway back and forth as we sang.

Sadly, about seven months after our arrival, the Catholic clergy were told they were to be sent elsewhere. We feared that they would be sent up to Mongolia or gassed like the Jewish people in Germany. Many of the other prisoners in China were walked up the Burma Road or into the interior of China with little food and terrible conditions. They often died of malaria and starvation.

Several of the clergy were our good friends, so Mother and I went about the crowd collecting their signatures in my little autograph book. A lot of the sisters were from Chowtsun in Shantung province. Others came from Peking and Tientsin. One of the sisters wrote to Mother: "They also serve who stand and wait—to serve! I shall always remember our camp duty with pleasure just because of the lovely people with whom I worked side by side." She must have been in the serving line with Mother.

One of my mentors, Father Gilkin, was a terrific artist and I spent many hours standing by his side and watching him paint and sketch parts of the camp. How I wished I could draw like this gentle man! Some of his sketches appear in Gilkey's book, but my favorite of a giant Chinese elm in front of the bachelor's dormitory may be lost forever.

The day they were to leave, we gathered in the largest dining hall to say our good-byes. It was an emotional moment with everyone talking at once. The place was packed with British, American, Dutch, Belgian, French, and Russian prisoners; all of us had grown so fond of the Catholic bishops, nuns, and brothers.

Where were they taking them? It was a mystery and each person had an opinion. Some thought they might be put into "work" camps as a lot of the military captured in China were. We had heard of the "ovens" used by the Germans to eliminate the Jews. Would this be their fate?

Suddenly, someone broke out with "God Bless America." We all joined in and the rafters of the dining hall shook with the sound as we belted it out! I have never felt such a surge of adrenaline and pride. The Jap guards cringed with the thought that we might use this surge of patriotism to start an insurrection. It was poignant to see their yellow faces turn pale as they gripped tightly to their bayonets.

Everyone felt a little better as we finished up with "Britannia" and the "Marseillaise" and shook hands all round. Often I think of those wonderful people and wonder what happened to them. We never heard from that group of clergy again, but I hold quite dear the tattered little autograph book with all their signatures in it.

Nosing around the barricaded Japanese barracks, Harry found himself a friend one day. A Japanese sergeant took a liking to him and invited him to sit and talk. After the first visit, Harry came back with a small packet of sugar. This culinary object was like a sack of gold to us. Harry was praised for his initiative and soon returned to visit the sergeant. To Mother's horror, he returned this time with the sergeant's well-worn uniform britches. "He just wants you to sew up the tear in the back of his pants," Harry pleaded. "Never!" screamed Mother. "Sew up the pants of the enemy? I'd rather die!" She took the britches and threw them into the corner of the room. "How dare he. What cheek," she muttered as she stormed off. It wasn't long though that she retrieved them from the corner and put a great big patch on the seat. "After all, the sergeant may take his anger out on Harry," she reasoned, "and I made a horrible job of the sewing anyway." She was truly British.

CHAPTER 10
PLAYS, GAMES, AND TERROR

Some of the prisoners lost a lot of weight by the second year, but even this travesty became a game. It was circulated about the compound that there would be a contest between the men to determine who had lost the most weight around their waist. Everyone turned out to watch the contest. The men lined up and, with jeers and jokes about their lovely figures, had their waists measured. One young man won by touching his fingertips in front of his abdomen and his thumbs behind his back. We laughed and cheered him on, but deep down we knew that things were getting pretty bad. How much longer could we hang on?

One of the things the British started was an amateur hour in the big auditorium. This building, which resembled a temple on the outside, was used for schoolrooms during the week; Catholic, Episcopal, and Baptist services on Sunday; and an entertainment hall on Saturday night. Even the Salvation Army members played familiar hymns, standing at the corner on Sunday night. "Rock of Ages" and "Nearer My God to Thee" were some of their favorites.

The shows on Saturday ranged from renditions on spoons, whistling, tap-dancing, and comedians, to plays and musical concerts. One man sang "Mammy" very well with his face blackened and dressed like Al Jolson. When he got down on one knee, opened his arms wide with white-gloved hands outstretched and wailed "Mammy," the whole crowd cheered. "A Christmas Carol" was very popular as December drew near. Tom was praised for the way he was "shooting" his cuffs into the air as he played the part of Tiny Tim.

It was something that kept the camp busy: auditioning and looking for talent. As the years dragged by, being confined grated on our nerves, especially the men. The Saturday show gave us something to look forward to and relieved the strain.

Harry got into the act, too. Doing a little two-step, he and a line of boys came out singing, "Mama's little baby loves shortnin' bread." Quite a feat for him, as Harry despised singing and was very shy. Too young to do my part, I watched with interest and enjoyed the laughs.

The ones who were really enthralled by the entertainment were the Japs. They insisted that the first two rows of seats be reserved for them and even though they understood very little English, there was always a lot of guffawing, clapping, and noisy laughing from their section.

Dressed in their brightly colored *yukata*, or silk robes, they were especially amused by the English banter, such as someone coming out with a crook to drag a bad comedian off the stage. Once an actor came onto the stage with a chamber pot and wove his way through a choral group as they were singing a classical piece: stopping at each of the singers and indicating that he wanted a donation, then peering into the pot with eyebrows raised and a quizzical look. This silly humor is so typical of the British, and the Japanese loved it.

In the summer, the sun scorched the campgrounds, making the dirt roads hot and dusty. Some likened it to a desert. Hopping from one shady place to another to keep my bare feet from burning on the dusty roads, I would make my way to the library a block away. Although we passed shoes down to others that fit them, in the summer it was just as easy to discard our too-tight shoes and go barefoot.

The library was my favorite place. It was made up of books that the internees had carried to the camp and donated. Several of them were children's books. There I discovered Florence Nightingale and Clara Barton and dreamed of being like them, caught up in a war and attending the bleeding, frightened soldiers holding my little lamp. Years later, Dad said to me, "I think you should study nursing." I agreed.

"One, two, buckle my shoe" we would chant as we jumped rope using a long piece of hemp we found lying around the Japanese barracks. I had a small group of friends that I hung around with (the first time that I had to deal with girls my age), and I was very shy. We signed each other's diaries and pledged that we would be true-blue to each other. Of course, that didn't last very long.

One of our favorite games was jumping rope, and we soon became accomplished at it. There was:

One Leaf in Time

Teddy bear, Teddy bear, turn around
Teddy bear, Teddy bear, touch the ground.
Teddy bear, Teddy bear, go upstairs,
Teddy bear, Teddy bear, say your prayers.
Teddy bear, Teddy bear, turn off the light.
Teddy bear, Teddy bear, say good night.

You did all the motions as you jumped the rope and said "Good night!" as you stepped out from under the swinging rope without it hitting you.

Other chants were "Grace, Grace, dressed in lace, went upstairs to powder her face" and "red hot pepper," where the rope went faster as the items got hotter. Hopscotch was also a favorite game, as was checkers, which we played with different-colored rocks.

One or two times the Dutch, Belgian, and English embassies sent care packages to their countrymen. When the food was consumed, the tin cans were discarded in the garbage cans at the end of each block. We found it lots of fun, rummaging through the garbage to collect the labels of these cans from different countries and exchange them with our friends, just as the kids do today with baseball cards.

Having no toys, television, or electronic games, we had to use our imaginations and improvise (something the children today don't do). Drawing paper dolls intrigued me. Spending hours, I would pretend my doll was attending a dance or going on a cruise, and I would dress her appropriately, even down to the shoes and parasol. There were no Barbie dolls with sequined dresses, hairbrushes, and high heels to be had, but my doll was just as classy with her crayoned outfits.

Most of the time I was a loner, having spent so much time without peers my age. But I slowly overcame my shyness with the help of our "club" and the people who spent so much time teaching and keeping us busy. Scouting was a big help, too. A large Scot, Miss Budd, started the Girl Guides, which is the European name for Girl Scouts. It was fun learning to tie knots, signal in Morse code (two arms stretched out for dash and one for dot), and even "camp out" in the camp, tying a blanket between bushes and building a little campfire over which I suspended my tin-can pot. Of course I had to be back in front of our rooms to be counted by nightfall, so I couldn't sleep over.

Christmases were hard times because we had no presents from "Santa," but we sang Christmas carols, had Christmas services and pageants, and tried to make each other a surprise gift. When I was ten, I sewed a small envelope-shaped purse out of a cotton handkerchief for my mother to keep her cloth bandages in. She used the strips of cloth to bind around her deformed foot, giving it padding. On the front I had embroidered a pink rose. "Oh, Sylvia, you did this all yourself!" she exclaimed in surprise. I was delighted that she used and kept it until it faded and finally fell apart.

Tom and Harry kept themselves busy around the camp. Tom claims that he and a chum sneaked out of the camp one day in a supply truck. The trucks were kept in the Japanese barracks but were not well guarded. "Geez, they don't watch these trucks like they should," noted Tom. "I bet we could climb into them and escape." So he and his friend, Frank, climbed over the barbed wire barricade and into a truck. "Duck under this tarpaulin, Frank. They won't see us and they'll drive right out of the camp." Their purpose was to get into Weihsien, but gee, where would they go from there?

They arrived in the city to find that beggars were starving in the streets. Some were eating paper and leaves to quell the gnawing in their stomachs. The Japanese had robbed them of all their food and murdered many of them. Scurvy and other diseases left them covered with sores, blind and lame. The place was teeming with heavily armed Japanese soldiers and it wasn't long before the boys were discovered. Tom insists that they were pulled out of the truck at gunpoint and sent back in an armored car. "Frank and I really thought we were goners and were we terrified!" I'm sure our parents were terribly frightened also, and Tom and Frank got severely reprimanded.

Our entrepreneur, Harry, kept himself busy stealing bricks out of the camp walls! He would work on them with a penknife until he got the bricks loose, usually picking a spot that was hidden by bushes or buildings. Then he would barter them to the internees who lived in the block rooms, and by the end of a year or so he had earned a big roll of Chinese bills. To the Japs' surprise, there were gray brick patios springing up in front of the blocks along the rows. Dad embellished ours by growing castor oil plants around it. The large dark-green leaves made a nice privacy hedge and a place to sit when our crowded rooms became unbearably hot in the summer.

One Leaf in Time

As the years dragged on, people became noticeably more lethargic and sickly. If it hadn't been for strong-willed men like Eric Liddell, who organized the children to play sports and keep active, we would have gone downhill, too. By the spring of 1945, he had started the Camp Olympics Games to keep us fit.

All the camp enjoyed the Olympics. It covered discus throwing, high jumping, wrestling, and track, as well as relay races and ballgames. Everyone turned out to compete and cheer their teams on. The long-distance race around the inner walls of the compound pooped me out but it was fun. I believe I came in last.

"Coming of age" had not been a problem with me until one day when I was lying in my top bunk feeling a little sick. The screen door opened and a friend of my brother strolled in saying he had come to visit Tom. I never liked the boy. He was a big, surly teenager who had gotten into trouble peeping into windows a few times, but we talked for a while. "Where are Tom and Harry and your parents?" he wanted to know. The next thing I knew he was standing on the lower bunk and groping into my shorts. "Get out or I'll tell my father!" I threatened, but he had me in a position where I could not get away from his probing hands and leering face. Luckily, I got my back to the wall next to my bunk and, with all my strength, kicked him in the face! He fell backwards, covering his bloody nose, and ran out the door. This encounter gave me a totally different view of the male gender.

From my top bunk there was another scary incident as I was falling asleep. The two-by-one-foot back window was located near the bottom of my bunk and, suddenly, I noticed something white creeping up the open screen. It looked at first like a large white hand and I was terrified that someone was trying to break into our room. A monster perhaps, trying to get me! "Mom!" I screamed. It turned out to be a large white rat, about the size of a boy's sneaker, with a trailing tail about a foot long. There was a pile of trash and old boards against our back wall and this large rodent had made a nest in it. The boys laughed at me, but my fear was so great that I would crawl into bed after that, covering my head with a blanket so I didn't have to look at that window. Dad went to the town council and complained that internees were throwing too many unused items outside, and soon the debris was removed. After that, camp authorities circulated an announcement: "All trash must be thrown away and nothing hoarded in the compound."

On the weekends, our incarcerators would get all spiffed up. Dressed in their fanciest yukata of yellow, green, and red silk, all perfumed and hair slicked back, they would walk down the dusty street in their wooden clogs. At the front gate, they would get rides into town to find some concubines to spend the night with or just to drink in the bars. Dad and a few of the other men would waylay them as they came back into camp and invite them into the rooms to sit and talk. It was a good way to get the news and, being lonely, the drunken soldiers had loose tongues. Besides, Dad kept a little black-market whiskey on hand to help. Many a time I saw a disheveled Japanese reeling out of our rooms late at night.

Some of us had found parts of weapons in our ceiling spaces and in the basements under the dormitories. Dad had found a pistol hidden over his room, but there were no bullets for it. Nevertheless, the men had been secretly plotting to overcome the Japanese when the time was right and the Communists were close enough to help us.

We knew the war was not going well for the Japs, often hearing their antiquated planes flying overhead sputtering and almost crashing. Japan was on the verge of giving up, but when? Surely they would be moving their battalions to the war-front soon, leaving our area of China unsupervised.

One dark night, two of the single men from the dormitory decided to make a break for it. With the help of a Chinese mercenary, they cut the electrified wires and hoisted themselves over the wall. They intended to join the Communist group upon hearing that Mao had moved his guerillas closer and was attacking the Japanese from the north.

As soon as they scaled the wall, sirens went off all over the camp. Armed Japanese, bayonets drawn, started rushing out of their living quarters. It was 2:00 a.m. and all of us came out, rubbing our eyes and wondering what was going on. Shouting and jabbing their bayonets at us, our jailers made us march to an open playing field.

"What are they going to do to us, Daddy?"

"I don't know, but I think that some of the people are missing. Stay close and do as they say. They seem very angry."

Lining us up in rows as to our housing in the blocks, they brought in machine guns that they set up in front of the group and trained on us. Then they went methodically down each row counting and counting again. It was a terrible loss of "face" to be missing one of their prisoners, and now, not only one, but two were missing! How would they report this to their superiors in Japan?

That was our scariest episode, as we thought they were going to shoot the lot of us. Instead, they kept us standing in rows, waiting for our fate until dawn, and then dismissed us back to our rooms. We did not know what had happened until Dad got a chance to talk to some of the dorm inmates. After that, we were all made to appear on the playing field at 4:00 p.m. each day and stand, with our armbands on, to be counted. If we were late, the whole block or dormitory had to stand an extra forty-five minutes. One of the internees was always late, so we usually spent a good part of the afternoon at roll call.

Chapter 11
RESCUED AT LAST

The school that was organized by the committee was rather haphazard. We sat in tiered rows of seats and, with the different subjects, changed places with the next grade level to another wing of the temple-like meeting building. One side covered mathematics, another covered English, and so on. The teacher in each section had to gear his instruction to the grade level of the children at that session. Again I learned algebra and long division.

We were blessed with a diversity of teachers; one even taught French. I remember singing "Frère Jacques" and "La Marseillaise" and getting the basics of the language. But history, which another teacher covered, was all British history, because he was English. There were King Arthur, Queen Elizabeth, Rufus the Great, and all the Henrys, including Henry VIII. Although I didn't get the best of grades, I enjoyed being introduced into an international and all-round experience and finally becoming a scholar.

About twice a week, we would all gather in this building and have music. Miss Budd, the beefy, ruddy-faced Scotch woman who also ran the Girl Guides, led us in song. Harry hated to sing, so he would just mouth the words and Miss Budd would put down her baton and move as close as she could to him. Then, cupping her ear with a fleshy hand, she would bend down to his face to hear his voice. The group would all titter, and poor Harry was so embarrassed his face would turn red.

"You take the high road and I'll take the low road and I'll get to Scotland before ye." It was August 17, 1945, and Miss Budd had us in full swing in our school building when it came: the sound of an American plane, different from the broken-down lawn mower sound of the Japanese air force, came steadily booming, louder and louder. We all dashed to the playing field, tumbling over each other in excitement and jumping up and down. Looking up to the sky with shaded eyes, we were enthralled by the sight of a huge, silver airplane as it swooped several times over our heads.

It flew so low that we could see the pilots sitting in the cockpit. Everyone was jumping, waving, and cheering, holding onto each other and laughing, then crying. This was it! We knew this was it!

Then out of the bowels of the B-17, seven parachutes unfolded one at a time. Armed American soldiers, looking like toy dolls, drifted into a cornfield next to the camp. Unfortunately, one of the men thought the top of the corn was the ground and with this misjudgment, broke his leg.

Throwing open the gates, the internees rushed out to meet U.S. Army Major Staiger and the six paratroopers who liberated us. Tom recalls that the Marines packed away their parachutes and, as he approached, they lay with weapons drawn, ready to tangle with the Japanese. The Japs, however, knowing the war was over, had piled their rifles in neat stacks and were standing in front of the guardhouse by the front gate, with their hands held over their heads. They gave in very passively and weren't about to argue with the U.S. troops! The only one missing was General Gesundheit. He evidently ducked out the back door, fearing reprisal.

Triumphantly, the jubilant internees carried in our rescuers (the Marine with the broken leg was given medical attention at our crude little hospital) and we stood up to give our heroes three "hurrahs!" before smothering them with questions and stories.

To our surprise, who should turn up during that week but the two men who had jumped camp about six months before? They had joined the Communists and, with dirt-smeared faces, proceeded to give us accounts of their escape, narrowly being caught by a band of Japanese reconnoiters, and their induction into the Communist army. They also told us that the Communists had chased the Japanese out of most of the cities and were all around the camp. Evidently they stayed on after that and fought with the guerillas.

Weihsien Camp: Building used for hospital, and one of the machine gun turrets

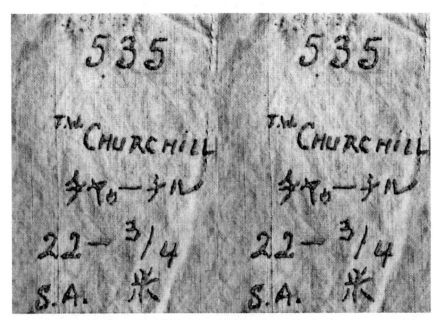

My brother Tom's armband. He was #535, living in block 22, rooms 3 and 4.

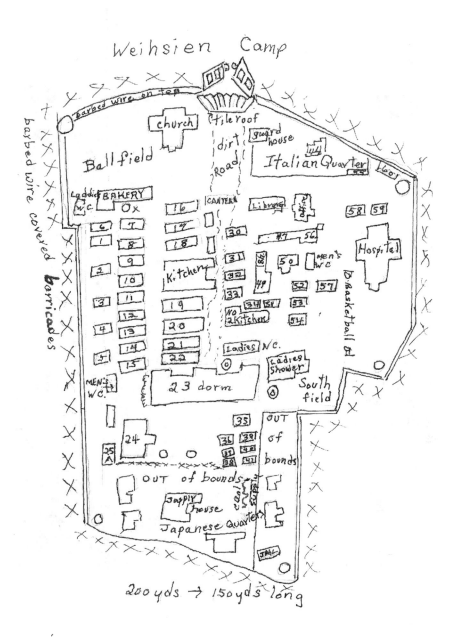

Map of Weihsien Camp, 1941–1945

Sylvia Prince

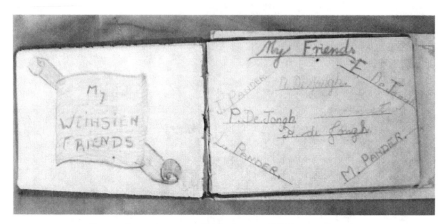

Items from Autograph book – my Weihsien friends

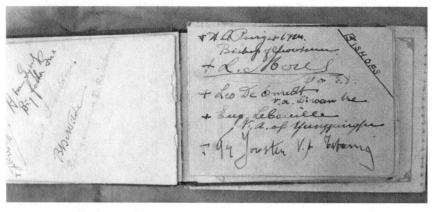

Items from Autograph book – "God bless Weihsien"

God bless our Weihsien
friends
Friends whom we love
Stand beside them and
guide them
Thru the night; with a light
from above
May we meet you, may we
greet you!
May we see you soon again
God bless our Weihsien
friends
Friends whom we love
Father Jan Joosg.

Items from Autograph book – "God bless Weihsien"

Items from Autograph book – letter with nuns' signatures

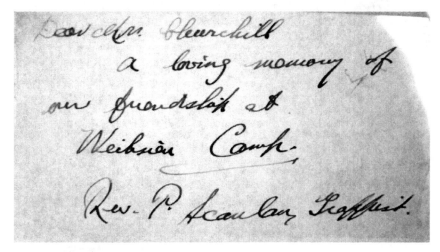

"God bless and keep you always"

Our supplier of Black Market items

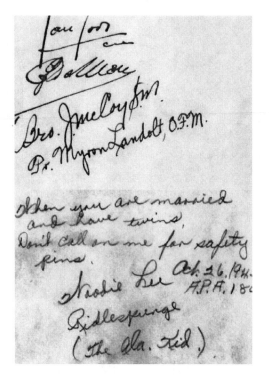

Army buddies aboard the U.S.S. *Lavaca*

U.S.S. *Lavaca*

U. S. S. LAVACA (APA-180)
C/O FLEET POSTOFFICE

TO ALL WHO SHALL SEE THESE PRESENTS, GREETING:

Know ye, that having participated in voyage on the
United States Ship LAVACA, attack troop transport, between the ports of Tsingtao, China and San Francisco,
U. S. A., and that having successfully competed for deck
space and in chow lines with innumerable Pacific Fleet
Sailors and Okinawa Marines, and that having demonstra-
ted a fine spirit of sportmanship and cooperation –

                Miss Sylvia Mary Churchill

        is appointed to the rate of

                SEAMAN (Honorary)

And is entitled to all the emoluments, honors, and respect due this high office, and shall be accepted and
acknowledged by all LAVACA Officers, Bluejackets, and
Marines as a SHIPMATE.

    Done this 24.5 day of October 1945, at Latitude
39°30'N and Longitude 180° E.W.

                WALTER S. GABEL
                Captain, USNR
                Commanding.

Certificate appointing me Honorary Seaman Lavaca

CHAPTER 12
MOVING DOWNSTREAM

After the first detachment of parachutists secured the camp, several more jeep-loads of soldiers and Marines were brought in to commandeer the Japanese and to sort out the evacuation of all the internees. The dense foliage had covered our camp so completely that it had taken them a month to find us. Trying to get transportation and locations for all of us was a big job. Most of the missionaries felt compelled to remain in China and continue their work in the provinces, but a lot of the businessmen knew that there would not be any of their jobs left in war-torn China, so they opted to go back to their homelands. Dad was given the option of taking us to the United States, with the help of the Red Cross, or going back to our house in Tientsin.

"What do you think, Ethel?" I remember him asking Mother. She had not been happy in China anyway, having been bossed by my two aunts and Grandma, and there was no guarantee that the house was not in a shambles after being occupied by the Japanese.

"You always wanted the children to become American citizens anyway, and this would be a wonderful opportunity for us to get to the United States," Mother reasoned.

So it was decided. What excitement, what curiosity about this new adventure! We couldn't wait to get started. But how would we travel over the Pacific Ocean to this new land?

After packing our bags and saying goodbye to all our Weihsien friends, Dad had to fill out several forms while we waited for trucks to carry us out of the city. During this time, the soldiers entertained the children with rides in their jeeps. Everyone piled on, but to my embarrassment, the tire under the fender that I was perched on went flat. The pounds I had gained must have done it, I thought. It really hurt to have everyone laughing at me as I jumped off.

Finally, the trucks arrived, and once again we made the trip to Weihsien. It was a dismal sight in the city to see beggars lying against the buildings, their sores full of flies, some trying to fill their stomachs with brown wrapping paper. I closed my eyes and turned my head into Mother's shoulder. She put her arm around me and drew me closer. What devastation to a quaint little city!

"Where are they taking us, Dad?" I asked.

"First they will take us to Tsingtao on the coast, and then, after all the paperwork has cleared, we will probably have to go to Shanghai in order to get a ship." Dad was familiar with all these cities along the coast of China, as he had often made sales trips there while he was working for COMIL.

It took us only a day to get to Tsingtao by train and the once-beautiful Edgewater Mansions where they housed us. This huge hotel, perched on the edge of the Pacific Ocean, was shaped like a crescent moon and boasted rounded balconies, stepped tiers, all facing out to the ocean. There must have been one hundred rooms—each one pillaged by the Japanese as they moved through the East Coast. Oriental carpets were stained and torn, walls were pitted and smeared with graffiti, and bare mattresses were piled in the corners. There must have been some beautiful pictures on the walls, but only the nails they hung from remained. It was a sad sight, but still better than our previous surroundings. The view from the balconies with the bright, blue Pacific Ocean extending out to what seemed eternity made up for the drabness of the rooms.

"Can we stay here forever, Mother?" I asked as we swam in the pristine lagoon next to the hotel. I was intrigued by the soft white sand and beautiful, small, pink shells. With the sun warming us, and the waves lapping at our knees, it seemed like heaven.

After two weeks, the Red Cross moved us again, with our meager clothing, to Shanghai. "Look, Tom, the buildings are all gray and go up so high you can barely see the sky." Shanghai was a really bustling city. The only relief from the austere business buildings were the flags and buntings draped occasionally with the firm's logo or name in Chinese. The rickshaws carried us through the city and to the docks. There we were introduced to our new living quarters: a troop transport named the USS *Lavaca*. Three hundred and ninety-two evacuees left Shanghai harbor on the USS *Lavaca* that day. It was October 11, 1945. There was a mixture of internees from several camps that the Japanese had in central China.

Our first stop was to be Okinawa, Japan, but after a day out to sea, we hit the tail end of a typhoon. That day we had gorged ourselves with a *foison* of food: pork chops, asparagus, fruits and juices, milk, and wonderful desserts. What a feast!

Just as we had our metal trays filled, the whole mess hall started to tip like a trick room in an amusement park. Then slowly, it tipped the other way. Everyone's food tray started sliding across the tables. People were eating out of their neighbor's tray as it slid past. Mashed potatoes, chops, and the entire marvelous accompaniment finally landed in a sloppy mess on the floor at the end of the tables while we gripped, white-knuckled, to a bar encircling each table.

"Whoa, what is happening?" Harry tried to grab his large piece of apple pie as it slid away. Not having our "sea legs" yet made it more unmanageable. The sailors were amused at our clumsiness. Trying to hold on to each other and gripping whatever seemed riveted to the floor, we finished our meal in haste. Poor Mom had a terrible time trying to stand up with her bad foot. Actually, we would have been better off if we hadn't dined so regally, as most of us got seasick and vomited all night. Some passengers stayed seasick for weeks.

When we came out on deck to go to our quarters in the bow of the ship, we could look down at our feet and see the ocean and look up to see the opposite railing of the ship above our heads. The wind was blowing the sea into your face with such strength you could barely stand up. Huge waves broke over the sides and swept over the deck.

"Hold on to this rope," Mom said, "so you won't lose your footing and get washed into the sea."

"I can't, I'm scared!" I said, but I slowly followed behind Mother and we reached the safety of our cabin. The following days were miserable as we fought off nausea with every roll of the ship and got into the routine of naval living.

"Peep—peep—peeeep!" Every morning we were awakened at 6:00 a.m. by the boatswain's whistle. Then the captain would give us announcements for the day or words of encouragement. "I'm really proud of the way that you weathered the storm last night. Hopefully, we can make the rest of the trip more enjoyable," or "There will be no more squirreling of food in your bunks. It encourages rats, and we have enough food, so do not try to save it. Have a good day." We were taking back portions of pies and cakes that we weren't able to consume, as we were so used to conserving our food and had missed these wonderful sweets during those three years. Trying to hide these goodies under our bunk mattresses was making a horrible mess.

The bunks that we slept in were like metal hammocks hung from the ceiling in tiers of three with barely enough room to turn over and certainly not enough room to sit up. Each night we rolled into these bunks, wrapped ourselves in a scratchy navy blanket, and were lulled to sleep by the rolling ship and the anchor sliding across the bow.

After the typhoon had passed, there was a large metal tub filled with orange sections for us to suck on. The Captain had ordered it put on deck to help us overcome motion sickness. He was a wonderfully kind and thoughtful man, often saying, "I want to make you as comfortable as possible on this old tub." Although some of the evacuees remained sick a long time, our family seemed to get over it pretty well. Tom, however, still cannot eat asparagus.

My friend Catherine and I soon found something to occupy our time. "Look, we can play house with these perfectly rolled ropes." Attacking the neatly coiled rescue ropes that the sailors had stacked in a corner of our deck, we sectioned out rooms: the kitchen here, the bedrooms there, using the ropes as our "walls." Well, did we get into trouble! The captain was furious as he blasted over the loudspeaker, "Whoever made this mess had better put it back in order *tout suite!*"

The next time we got into trouble was on Navy Day. In celebration, the captain had assigned a sailor to take us on a tour of the ship. Mother didn't go, but a whole crowd of evacuees followed behind our escort, who was explaining the procedures in the different parts of the ship. They fired off the big antiaircraft guns, showed us the bridge, and had us following this seaman all over the ship.

Well, Catherine and I were not paying attention when he announced that the tour was over so, like a couple of rats, we kept following the Pied Piper. To our embarrassment, he led us down into the sailor's quarters in the belly of the ship. As we climbed down the steep metal stairs we were suddenly confronted with about forty sailors sitting, standing, and lying in their bunks with nothing on but their underwear! We burst out laughing.

"Come on Catherine, let's get out of here," I gasped, as we quickly turned and struggled back up the ladder, hoping we had not been seen.

Harry and Tom really admired the sailors and the work they did on the ship. Sometimes they were allowed to help with the chores, like polishing the railing. Harry found a virtual oasis of business with the sailors and the Marines, who, because they were headed home to their families, were eager to swap whatever they had for his Chinese money. Touting the "perfect souvenir," Harry had his pockets filled with American money and candy bars in no time. No wonder he had to go to the dentist as soon as we were settled.

The Lucky *Lavaca*, whose logo was a big cow with a sailor hat on, pulled into Okinawa about a week after we left Shanghai. It was rumored that we were to pick up a load of Marines who had been fighting there. Everyone strained to see as the stringer pulled up and our crew lowered the Jacob's ladder. Dressed in fatigues, with their sunburned faces still smudged from the rigors of war, the Marines assailed the knotted rope ladder in rows of eight to ten. This was their trip home and it showed in their eager faces as they agilely climbed up the ship. On their backs, their packs and bedrolls—all that they cared about. "Look, Mother, there is a tiny monkey clinging to that marine's back. Isn't it cute?" Sure enough, one of the Marines was allowed to board with his new friend and pet.

After they were settled in, we continued on our voyage with a full ship. The Marines were put in the stern of the ship with the male evacuees and were given strict orders not to encroach on the women in the bow. They ate in the mess hall after us, but we all enjoyed coming on deck during the day and basking in the sunshine and watching the ocean.

One afternoon, after lunch, with my usual tardiness, I was climbing the mess hall ladder when I looked up to see the doorway blocked by a blond-haired willow of a man. His raw-boned jaw collapsed into a luxuriant smile as he leaned back on the metal railing. "Well, hi-yah little gal, let me give you a hand up!"

A bronzed, callused hand reached down to mine and I felt the strength of a well-trained arm lifting me up the last steps. "Marine Corps Sgt. Lewis Hornsby here," he snapped with a brisk salute. "What's your title?"

CHAPTER 13
LIFE ON THE LUCKY *LAVACA*

There were casual meetings on deck with Lewis that led to a warm bond between us. Movies were shown on the aft deck at night, and Lewis would sit with his knees pulled up and, leaning my back against them, I would sit ensconced with his field jacket wrapped around me. It was so exciting for me to see Charlie Chan, The Three Stooges, and Lucille Ball in their captivating episodes, as the only movie I had seen up to this time was one in which Laurel and Hardy were stretched and scrunched, and to me it wasn't funny. Being only six at the time, it just gave me nightmares.

Now we had become good friends: a young Marine, longing for the comfort of home and family, and a young girl longing for security and a home, period.

As he arranged his jacket closer around me at the ship's rail, I turned and looked up into his sunken dark eyes.

"What was the war like, Lewis?" He stared down at me for several minutes.

"I really hate talking about it," he finally mumbled in a low voice. "We were attacked by mortar fire the minute we hit the beach. I turned around and my buddy, Jack, had half his head blown off. The captain kept screaming for us to advance, but he got it, too. We were like robots, just doing what we had been trained to do and inside hoping that it wouldn't be our turn next."

He drew me up to him as if the warmth of my body would chase the vision away, like a frightened child holding on to his teddy bear. I wished that I could.

Okinawa, a large island located between Japan and Formosa, was the site of one of the bloodiest campaigns of World War II. Led by their general, from April until July 1945 the American troops tried their best to oust the Japanese from their stronghold. Kamikaze planes made suicidal strafes of the U.S. ships carrying our troops, and many of our ships were sunk. About 12,500 Americans lost their lives; 110,000 of the Japanese soldiers died, and 7,800 of their planes went down. Also, of the people living in Okinawa, 60,000 were killed. What price war?

Lewis's face had become a frozen mask, and the muscles of his neck and jaw had tightened as if I had hit a very sensitive nerve. Earlier, he had told me his comrades called him "Horny," derived from his last name. "What does that mean?" I'd asked him naïvely. "Let's not go there," he replied with a wry smile. "It's not very nice." So I settled on calling him "Lewis."

"What is Alabama like?" I queried.

"Well, Dad has a small peanut farm there. Actually I should be home helping him dig the crops right now. Reckon he'll tease me about trying to get out of work again. Gee, I miss him, the nice flat farmland and the live oaks in our front yard." His muscles relaxed, and I could see I had conjured up more pleasant thoughts.

The captain tried his best to make the journey more bearable. He had the carpenter (I believe with Dad's help) build a shuffleboard court. There were all sorts of plays and amateur shows. The crew formed a band with a trombone, piano, trumpet, drums, clarinet, saxophone, and violin, and found a civilian passenger who could play the guitar.

The *Lavaca* began taking on the look of a cruise ship; considering they didn't have much time to practice, the shows were pretty good.

The Marines and sailors (some of whom had boarded in Okinawa) were all as kind as they could be. If a woman or child was struggling to step over the high doorsteps that led out on deck or climbing down the steep ladders, the willing arm of one of the servicemen was always outstretched to help. By October 24, we were all getting into the routine when the captain surprised us with a special ceremony making us all honorary shipmates.

Then he put our names on certificates. Dad, Mom, Tom, and Harry were appointed the rate of "coxswain." I was only given the title of "seaman," possibly because of my age, or maybe because the captain remembered the episode of the ropes. As the ceremony ended, a large wave swept over the side of the ship, drenching us all. "Well, that makes the initiation complete," chortled the captain in his Texas drawl.

One morning, the *Lavaca* crossed the International Date Line, an imaginary line drawn down the middle of the Pacific Ocean from the

Aleutians to New Zealand. When you crossed it, you lost a day. One of the sailors had his birthday on that day, so, to celebrate the sailor's double birthday, the captain had a big party for us. There was lots of cake and band music. Everyone had a good time.

Finally, on November 4, the captain alerted us to the fact that we would be sailing into San Francisco Bay the following morning. We had just left an overnight stay in Honolulu, Hawaii, where the first American ships had been bombed, and, although we were not allowed to disembark, the somber remembrance was enough to bring back the devastation of war. Here, some of the sailors aboard were let ashore for R&R (rest and relaxation).

We were elated with the captain's news. What excitement! I could barely sleep. We gathered our belongings together and spoke in hushed voices. What would America be like? Would the people be friendly? All sorts of questions went through my mind.

The next morning, November 5, we dressed hurriedly and climbed up to the deck before the sun came up. A heavy fog covered the water as we all rushed to the side of the ship. The salt sea air permeated our nostrils and the only sound was the slap, slap, slap of our ship as she broke through the waves. Mother had to hold on to the back of the boys' shirts as they leaned out over the railing, trying to see through the blanket that surrounded us. Everyone stood tense, craning their necks and holding their breath, seemingly afraid that they would destroy the moment by breathing.

"I think I see something!" Tom shouted. "Yes, it is." Straining our eyes, we began to discern a structure breaking through the fog. Little by little, we could make it out. First the girders, then the beautiful arch. Yes, it was—the Golden Gate Bridge! Little cars, like tiny ants, were streaming across the trellised span of steel. Everyone screamed with joy, pointing and hugging each other. As the old *Lavaca* glided under the bridge and into the San Francisco harbor, the sun came out, dissipating the fog. Then came the high-pitched bosun's whistle, followed by the announcement we had all been waiting for. "Congratulations shipmates," boomed the captain, "You have reached America!"

CHAPTER 14
NEW PILGRIMS

"Sorry for the rain, folks." A chubby Red Cross representative met us as we disembarked. We were checked over quickly and carried by bus to a small hotel at the waterfront. The clerk at the desk seemed quite uninterested in our demeanor or origin. The Red Cross was paying the bill, and that was all that mattered.

After our small trunks had been stored in the room, we were eager to explore the city. "Look how the roads go up and down over steep hills," observed Tom. "And the stores are jammed so close together," said Harry. We were afraid to go too far in case we got lost, but what fun! "Look at all the pretty jewelry and clothes in the store windows!" I marveled. Mother looked longingly at them, too. Her threadbare clothes, once fashionable, hung in rags about her.

The misty rain touched lightly on our hair and eyelashes as the pungent, salty smell of the sea rose from the bay. Now and then you could hear the moan of the bay buoys alerting ships to the shoals around San Francisco Bay.

Street trolleys clanged down the steep streets and glided up the next rise with ease, their occupants hanging on to the polished brass door poles and leaning out of the windows. "Can we ride one, Daddy?" I asked.

"No, we don't have money for that. Maybe someday." His foot slipped on the wet cobblestones. Annoyed, he muttered, "Let's find someplace to eat!"

Chinatown was a jungle of discarded cardboard boxes and refuse-strewn sidewalks. The garbage was swept from the stores and out into the streets, leaving small piles of muck for the passerby to step over. An acrid odor of sewer exuded from every grate, while puffs of cooking oil and fried foods regaled our nostrils as we passed the doorways. The storefronts were decorated with elaborate dragons and colorful lanterns.

"Let's stop here; the menu is reasonable." Dad ushered us into a red painted doorway and gave Mother his arm. She had been limping, as the rubber wedge in the sneaker for her bad foot had worn down, causing a large blister on what was already a painful appendage.

The meal went well. Dad spoke Cantonese to the proprietor, and he took a little off the bill. They enjoyed a long conversation about the places where they had lived and their experiences in China.

"Stay here and let me talk to the authorities." Dad, armed with our passports, was up early the next day to arrange our passage to New England and his hometown of Plymouth, Massachusetts. When he returned, he was jubilant! "The Red Cross will pay for our passage on the Santa Fe Railroad to Chicago. It will cost six hundred dollars, which I have to pay back in two years." Dad was not afraid of work and he planned to look up old relatives who might steer him into a job. "I'll get it paid in a year, probably." Little did he know that most of his relatives had died, and the cancer that was growing rapidly in his pancreas would soon be sapping his strength and abilities.

"What a big train! The engine is awesome." Tommy, lugging the suitcases, stopped to admire the iron and steel monster hissing steam onto the platform, its yellow and blue body glistening in the sun. "Look at all the passenger cars. They must stretch across America," murmured Harry in wonder. All the noise just made me nervous. "All aboard!" called the conductor. We pulled out of San Francisco on November 10.

Noses pressed against the window, we watched as the panorama of the desert sauntered by with its golden mesas and flat-topped plateaus. "Look at those rocks, Harry," I said. "They look like castles, and that one makes a bridge. How neat!" Who knew that later on in life, I would come back with my family to explore those canyons and national parks in an Apollo motor home.

The terrain soon changed as we rumbled across the mesquite-strewn ranches of Texas. We pressed our noses against the glass for such a long time that it made me giddy. Then, with an excited "look at that cowboy!" or "tumbleweed" or "longhorn cattle" from Tom and Harry, I would have to rush back to my spot.

The trip was long, taking about two days and two nights. Cramped together, we slept in spells. I never saw Dad more excited and expectant. He was puffed out like a blowfish.

From Chicago, we transferred to a train to Boston and then finally down to Plymouth, arriving November 14. The trip was uneventful except that we were tired—bone tired. Each of us felt that Dad had commandeered us to this unfamiliar town with no one to greet us, nowhere to stay, and nothing to eat. To add to the depression, it was raining and cold—the typical New England raw cold that seeps into your bones and dulls the luster of living.

There we stood on the platform in semi-darkness, as it was six o'clock in the evening; our suitcases, all our worldly possessions, were strewn at our feet. Soaking wet, we waited while Dad hunted for a taxi. What a sorry lot we were!

Somehow we ended up at the Pilgrim hotel overlooking Plymouth Rock (the rock that the pilgrims first stepped onto at the water's edge as they landed). It was off-season, so Dad got a pretty good rate. The next day he was going to scout the town to find us a more permanent residence.

"I've found a house we can rent in a town called Manomet, just south of here," he announced a day later. "Mr. Flank, the owner, will allow us to move in without a down payment, and he trusts us to pay him the month's rent as soon as I get a job. So get the kids packed up, Ethel."

Dad had also tried to locate relatives, but the only ones he could find were Ezra Dimon and his sister, Helen Whitten. "We must try to visit them. They are my cousins," he said.

Unfortunately, when we did, we found them very frail and living in a rustic old house on the edge of town. Aunt Helen's hands were terribly deformed with arthritis, and I saw, with amazement, that she had no washing machine. All of their week's clothing was soaking in a five-foot porcelain washtub. She was going to scrub and wring out all that laundry by hand! My heart instantly went out to this woman. "Let me help with your washing," I must have said to her, because Aunt Helen immediately took a liking to me. Her winsome blue eyes, set back in bony sockets, glistened as she served us tea. (When Aunt Helen died, she left me a large brown raccoon coat and a lovely old Tiffany-style etched-glass lamp—all she had that was precious to her.)

We moved to Manomet on November 20. The house Dad had found was near the ocean—a big, wooden Cape Cod style with very little insulation. There was a neat landing about three steps up, which either turned to a flight of stairs up to four bedrooms or down three steps to a small bathroom and adjoining kitchen. I loved the bench on the landing where I could sit and read and watch the loblolly pines.

In the living room sat a huge kerosene stove. Its black iron hulk took up most of the room. The boys and I had the job of feeding it every day with kerosene that was kept in a drum in the back of the house. The five-gallon jug we had to fill was cumbersome to wrestle from the shed, haul up the back stairs, and turn over into the stove receptacle. I can still hear the "glug, glug, glug!" as the hungry monster consumed its kerosene.

Although this space heater warmed the lower rooms very well, there was only a grate in the ceiling by which the heat circulated to the bedrooms above. As a result the rooms were always cold and drafty.

Sam Flank would come over every evening and start arguing politics with Dad. Neither side won, but as the argument got more heated, their voices would rise in pitch until they were shouting at each other. Dad called him "Comrade Flank" because he was so enthralled with communistic concepts. Anyway, one day I brought my homework down to the living room, but I could not concentrate with the noise going on. "Shh!" I said inadvertently, just as Dad was saying, "Sam, Communism is just another way for a dictator to bleed his people." Suddenly, all eyes were on me. "Go to your room! What are you doing down here anyway?" Dad shouted, pointing with a gnarled finger to the stairs.

It was no use explaining that I had come downstairs because it was so cold upstairs my legs were like frozen blocks of ice. Slamming my book shut, I hurried back upstairs with the guilt of a child being punished.

It was hard for Dad to find work. At first he had to walk to Plymouth over the Pine Hills, an eight-mile hike over uphill terrain, and come home at night carrying an armload of groceries. Finally, he got enough money to buy a Model T Ford. We were ecstatic! Off we would go to the school football games as soon as Tom got his license, our feet hanging out of the windows, dressed in school colors, penny loafers, and bobby socks. Tom and Harry both played on the team. Harry was the official kicker. On the back of his torn pants, the school had patched a big "X," so every time he was called in to kick the goal I would shout, "X marks the spot, Harry!" He never missed a goal either.

Poor Dad tried several jobs before he finally became manager of an Esso filling station. He sold roofing, tires in a Dunlop tire store, and Guardian service ware that entailed his giving dinner parties. The boys and

I had to assist him by cooking the dinner and washing up afterwards while Dad gave his presentation. The pots, made of aluminum, were heavy and difficult to clean, but they did cook with small amounts of water, retaining a lot of the vitamins. Finally, after Dad dropped one of the glass lids, trying to demonstrate that it was shatterproof, and it smashed into a million pieces, he quit that job. The boys and I were not disappointed!

Dad was very protective as a parent. At fifteen, I decided all my friends were wearing lipstick so I should, too. Dad evidently still wanted to keep his little girl unblemished. "Go blot some of it off," he demanded. Unwillingly, I went upstairs and blotted my lips. "Still too much, wipe some more off." Dad kept saying this until, after four trips, there was no more lipstick on my lips. "That's better," he said with a wry smile.

When I was able to date, he always wanted to know where I was going and how late we would be. As the boy arrived, Dad would sit him down and cross-examine him, and when we came back home, Dad would be sitting up, waiting for me.

After Dad died and I was in nursing school, I was dating a Norwegian boy who was stationed on the Cape in the Air Force. One weekend I brought Ray home to meet my mom. It was a lovely day, Mom gave her approval, and we were on our way back to Boston when Ray's old jalopy started to billow out steam. "Darn, my radiator has run dry," he cursed.

Looking over, I noticed that the cemetery where Dad was buried was located at the next turnoff. "There are a lot of taps in the cemetery, Ray. Let's turn off here and I'll show you," I said. The next thing I knew we were climbing the hill up to Dad's grave site and the only tap we found was across from it. I looked over to Dad's gravestone and got an eerie feeling. Had Dad brought us up to see him so he could be introduced to my date? His presence was so strong that I whispered, "Hurry up, Ray, let's get out of here!"

One of the most important things Dad taught me was to concentrate on the difficult parts of life and not to worry over the simpler problems. I was cleaning the large windows in our dining room one day, which was my job, while Dad leaned casually on the doorjamb watching me. "Sylvia," he said, "if you clean the corners first, the center will take care of itself." Of course, being a teenager, I just gave him a glare, but the words have stayed with me as I tackle difficult tasks first and let the easier ones slide into place through life.

Although Japan surrendered on August 14, 1945, the mode of life in America had changed. Americans had to tighten their belts from the throes of war. Gasoline, housing, and food were hard to come by. By 1947 the government announced the end of rationing sugar and meat, but scrap metal was still in demand. After we became friendly with the other teenagers in Manomet, we formed a community center called "Teentown," which we supported by collecting metal (like brass piping and old hubcaps), newspapers, and glass bottles. From the money we raised, we were really proud when a ping-pong table and jukebox graced our basement quarters. "Blueberry Hill" and "Dozey Dotes" floated out of the big, multicolored hulk of plastic as the black discs slipped into place and the robotic arm moved smoothly over their surface. The boys were too bashful to dance, but we chatted and enjoyed the music.

Dad enrolled us into school first thing. "Harry can stay back in the sixth grade so that Sylvia will not be overwhelmed by attending school on her own," the school superintendent said. He believed it would be better for me having the company of my brother. Unfortunately, for Harry, it was complete boredom. We went to a little white wooden schoolhouse in Manomet while Tom got to ride the school bus to Plymouth and take interesting subjects and sports. Harry found the math and English far too simple, but we were both challenged in history. Whereas we had been well schooled in English and French history (various King Henrys, Edwards, and Rufus the Red), the stage turned to the landing of the pilgrims, Governor Bradford and Priscilla Alden and the various Indians who befriended them in their first cold winter. It was a whole New World, literally, with Salem witch hunts and Boston tea parties. The other problem was our speech. Although we spoke English, there were several words that had different meanings in their translation. For example, I made the mistake of asking Henry, the boy next to me, for his "rubber," as I had to erase something on my paper. He looked at me in surprise and said, "WHAT?" then broke into peals of laughter. Later I learned that what this promiscuous sixth grader had in mind was a condom.

Each Friday, Dad would give us a dime to buy a war stamp that we pasted in a little book until we got enough to buy a bond. Dad could barely afford it, but he was terribly proud of his country and wanted to help bring it back after the war. We stood in line at school and had our fingernails, hair, and teeth checked while buying the stamp. Later, one of my friends, who had been a teacher, said she wished they would keep up this hygiene procedure in schools today.

Mom, the boys, and I were not "Americans" as yet. Because we children were born outside the United States and did not come to the United States before we were nine, we had to be naturalized along with Mother, who had kept her British citizenship while in China. It took us six long years before attaining our citizenship. We had to learn the history of America, know the presidents, the ten amendments to the Constitution, the Preamble, and the Pledge of Allegiance. Then the authorities monitored our whereabouts and behavior as a citizen while in the country.

"Sorry, Sylvia, somehow we lost all of your records." This blow came from one of the officials in the immigration department. I was struck numb! Then I started to cry (my usual habit when I'm angry or frustrated). "Don't worry," he assured me, "we'll get right on it." It was not until I was in my first year of nursing school, however, that the paperwork was finally in order. When I finally got to raise my right hand and recite the Pledge of Allegiance, the emotion was overwhelming. We stood up tall with lumps in our throats and, after all those years of being scrutinized, were proud to finally be "Americans!"

Chapter 15
SETTLING IN

The most important thing that the camp taught us was not only a person's love of those around him, but his need of their support. So many people draw in their breath and gasp, "You were in a concentration camp? Oh—you poor thing!"

Actually, living in such confined quarters, we learned to lean on each other and coexist. Strength was gained from the consolation and help of others, whether they were Jewish, Catholic, Protestant, or Buddhist. Our weird conglomeration of businessmen, clergy, and executives soon got to mesh and work as a unit. (There were no military, as the Japanese had killed or captured the few American Marines stationed in Tientsin and Peking. These cities were soon changed to Tianjin and Beijing.)

After we arrived in Manomet, Mother tried desperately to nurture a new circle of friends. During the summer, she ambled down to the beach on hot afternoons and mingled with the other mothers. Often, she brought a note pad so she could jot down recipes and bits of information on housecleaning. Prior to this she'd had no exposure to these arts.

Her best friend was Margaret Stenott, a big, bright-eyed Irishwoman whose jet-black hair always looked like she had caught her finger in a toaster. Margaret was jolly, heavily structured, and full of Irish cracks. On one occasion, Mother and Margaret were sitting on a beach blanket when two men from New York came down and spread their blanket next to them. At that time "gays" were not very prevalent, or they kept secluded. Dressed in scanty, thong-like bikinis, they started practicing ballet steps on the sand. Then they proceeded to prance down to the ocean, arms waving like butterflies. "Oh, I bet we'll see their peckers stand up when they hit that ice cold water," Margaret chortled with an impish grin and wide-open eyes. Mother laughed, "They may even lose those pants!"

"I'm going to have a baby," Mom announced out of the blue. Our first reaction was, "You have to be kidding!" Mother was over forty and all literature at that time claimed a woman who got pregnant at that age was at risk. She always was in good health, but gosh, we were all teenagers and Dad was still struggling to keep his brood fed. Why another one?

Still, as the reality sank in, I was excited to think I would soon have a baby brother or sister to play with and spoil. Abigail was born on February 18, 1947, at the Jordan Hospital in Plymouth, Massachusetts. A well-seasoned woman doctor realized that the baby was breech. With one mighty twist of her hands around my Mother's abdomen, she turned the baby right side up. Mother and I were shocked, but the old doctor just grunted and remarked, "Now, let's go have this baby." It wasn't that easy for Mom, who stayed in labor for at least ten hours. Abigail was born pink, loud, and lovely, with no defects or problems.

It was a whole new life with a baby at home. I'd come home from school and proudly walk my sister in her pram up and down the streets of Manomet while Mother got an hour's rest. Saturdays were spent washing laundry, mostly diapers, feeding the wet clothes through a mangle, an instrument with two rollers that pressed the water out of the clothes.

As Abigail got bigger, we would lock her out on the porch while we did the vacuuming. Poor thing, she would have her red nose pressed against the window, crying her heart out, and Mom and I would just laugh.

"Give me your tired, your poor." The words rang out to the rafters of our auditorium. How well I could remember when we were the tired and poor. It was June of 1952 and Harry and I were graduating from high school. Tom had graduated the year before. During the assembly, our class was to sing the Lord's Prayer and the inscription on the Statue of Liberty. "Your huddled masses longing to breathe free." It conjured up a vision of us arriving on the USS *Lavaca* and walking down that gangplank. How apropos to have it coupled with the Lord's Prayer, which we sang with much gusto. Nowadays it would not be permitted in the school. (How times have changed.)

One Leaf in Time

At the same time as I was graduating from high school, James Rex Prince from Union, New Jersey, was throwing his cap into the air and getting his diploma from Tufts College in Boston. Stripping off their graduation gowns, they were in full ROTC gear and in the Navy. From there he was posted to the cruiser USS *Worcester* as an ensign and shipped to the Mediterranean. Assigned to the crypto room, he carried top-secret material in a briefcase, often chained to his wrist. North Korea and South Korea were at war and the United States had stepped in to assist the South Koreans, who were being taken advantage of.

After World War II, Japan had to leave Korea, which it had occupied. The northern half, separated by the 38th parallel, was to be controlled by the Soviet Union, and the southern half by the United States. I was in high school when the North Korean troops first slipped across the 38th parallel and started antagonizing their neighbors in South Korea. President Truman called on the American people to defend this territory, and in 1951 the Korean War began. Tom and Harry both enlisted. Tom joined the Marines and Harry joined the Army a year later.

China, afraid to anger the Russian Bear, joined in with the North Koreans. It was a devastating battle for the American troops, who were not used to fighting an enemy who could hide in tunnels and thatched huts with various disguises. Again, we got into a battle we were not prepared for.

The hostilities ended in 1953 with a truce to be settled at an international conference. More than a million civilians had been killed and many of our soldiers, quite a few of them African Americans, lost their lives or were MIAs (missing in action).

One of the MIAs was an Air Force pilot, a native of Shenandoah, Virginia, who crashed his B-29 into a North Korean mountain in April 1951. His remains were not found until 2007, when a group staging an archaeological dig got to this remote spot and found his plane. About 8,100 Americans are still missing, and the search goes on to the tune of $50 million a year. When remains are found, DNA samples identify them, and it gives the families closure.

Luckily, my brothers never were deployed to Korea. Dad wrote to them constantly, always afraid that they might be sent to the war. I tried to send messages when I could, but I had started at Massachusetts General Hospital School of Nursing and had problems of my own.

Harry did tickle me when he wrote home one time and said the way he kept out of trouble when they were looking for a "volunteer" was to pick up a broom and start sweeping!

Chapter 16
MASSACHUSETTS GENERAL HOSPITAL

After I graduated, Dad said, "I think you should study to be a nurse." It was my childhood dream, so I agreed. Even though it was a little trouble getting me in with a C in Latin, Dad enrolled me in the Massachusetts General Hospital School of Nursing. "It's a very good school, Sylvia. I hope you will do well there."

Mass. General (or MGH) was built on the banks of the Charles River in 1811 because it was convenient to transport patients in boats. Now the riverbanks have been filled in and the hospital is buried inside the city with larger buildings surrounding it. Its first claim to fame was the use of ether for a major operation; this groundbreaking use of anesthesia took place in 1846 in the Bulfinch Building, the original hospital facility designed by American architect Charles Bulfinch. Ether had been used by a dentist earlier, but until Dr. William T. G. Morton introduced its use for more complicated surgical operations, patients had to be drugged or sedated with alcohol.

Boston was scary—no, terrifying—to me at first. I had a roommate who was a social butterfly and insisted the other *probies* (as we were called) stop by and visit on their way past our first-story room. Each probie was supposed to get a "big sister" to help in adjustment, but mine was pregnant and could only send me a note wishing me "Good Luck!" I never saw her.

Needless to say, I flunked anatomy and was dragged in to see Miss Sweeper, the nursing director. After a teary explanation of my circumstances and the dream I had of following in Nightingale's footsteps, Miss Sweeper said, "I'll give you another chance, but you'll have to come back to the September class." I was so relieved because I knew Dad was going to kill me. To my surprise, Dad gave me a lecture and only cautioned that this time I had better do well or find a job. The second time around was better. I was put in the Thayer Building, which was connected to the hospital and allowed us to reach classes, cafeteria, etc. in the main building by way of an underground tunnel. Miriam, a tall, mature student, was in a room across the hall and we often studied together. Still, there were times when we had fun.

Although the Harvard Medical students would barely deign to look at us, we all fantasized a date with one of them. We sang songs in our kitchen and one I made up went like this:

We're poor little probies who have gone astray,
Baa, baa, baa.
Harvard med students off on a spree,
They sure know their anatomy.
Lord, have mercy on such as we.
Baa . . . Baa . . . Baa.

We gradually stepped up from bedpans, back rubs, and making beds (it took me several sessions to get that rubber draw-sheet tight enough to bounce a nickel a foot high) to working on the floors, giving baths, changing bandages, doing treatments, and giving medicines.

At first, being shy, I found it difficult to converse with the patients, but understanding the patients and their diseases made me more comfortable. My first patient had trichinosis, a now rare disease found in raw pork, caused by a parasite. It was easy to practice giving a back rub to this handsome young man.

A small Asian laundryman was one of my saddest patients. He had been consuming a six-pack of beer each night in his lonely apartment after working all day. The alcohol had caused esophageal veins along the inside walls of the esophagus to rupture and even though the doctors had tried compressing the blood vessels with an instrument called a Sengstaken-Blakemore tube, the poor frightened little man was bleeding to death. I could do nothing but hold a kidney basin to his chin while he vomited blood in spurts.

Some of the blood invariably spattered over my white starched apron, and the poor soul would lift his head and sputter, "I sollie, I sollie!" I felt so helpless and frustrated as I wiped his forehead with a cold compress. That night, he passed away.

By 1955, we had taken our training at the Boston Lying-In Hospital in obstetrics. Working with mothers and babies was a refreshing and interesting new experience, but when I got back to MGH, depressing news awaited me.

Dad had been diagnosed with Addison's disease while I was in my second year at Mass. General. This disease, afflicting the kidneys and causing jaundice, was diagnosed in President Kennedy while he was in office but the diagnosis was kept secret. Even Vice President Johnson thought Jack Kennedy had an old back injury when he needed help in walking.

Every weekend that I was home, I noticed Dad drinking bottles of Di-Gel, an antacid. Finally, he could stand the pain no longer and was admitted to the Bulfinch Building at Mass. General. I visited him between classes. He was still in a lot of pain and the Cortisone pellets they were inserting under his skin were actually making the cancer, which was really what he had, worse. Poor Dad, he couldn't sleep between the pain and a ward full of other men all groaning. The medical men didn't want to release him to the surgical doctors, so his fate see-sawed back and forth.

The weekend after he was admitted, I was walking by the surgery board that hung in the main hall of the White Building. (There were about twelve operating rooms in the hospital, so they had to be scheduled on this board each day.) My eye caught "Exploratory Laparotomy" listed in one of the rooms and the patient was from Bulfinch. It did not list the name, age, or condition but I knew immediately, "It must be Dad."

Racing up to the amphitheater that overlooked the scheduled OR room, I sat numb as they wheeled Dad in on a gurney and proceeded to prep him. Ashamed that I had not visited him that morning, I sat transfixed, as a saucy young Harvard medical student strode into the room kicking off his loafers as he proceeded to gown. "Well, look at this yellow-skinned Chinaman!" Dad was jaundiced due to the pancreatic cancer. Normally, his skin was brown and leathery from so much exposure to the sun. "Isn't he pretty?"

As he sliced into Dad with flourishes and jokes, I began to hate this man. It wasn't long before I was reduced to tears as this cocky young man found cancerous lesions on every organ of Dad's body. "I'll cut everything out from the esophagus to his lower intestine and sew him back up. There is no way this man will live more than a few weeks." He handled it like a boy fixing a flat tire on his bicycle, so casually. I wanted desperately to turn on the speakerphone and give this doctor a chiding, but if they were aware of my presence I would have been expelled from school. That is not what Dad would have wanted!

Running to the public telephone, I called Tom and gave him all the gruesome news, sobbing between each sentence as tears streamed down my face. Harry was still in the Army, so I couldn't reach him, and Abigail was only six years old. Tom would tell Mother. What else could I do? My mind swirled and my heart pounded as I made my way, distraught, to the cafeteria in hopes of finding some buddies who would console me. To my surprise, the same medical student was in line, loading up his tray with a sumptuous lunch. My urge was to accost this prima donna, but it was likely he would only sneer if I confronted him. I could only hope that he flunked his last exams and never got to practice medicine.

Dad died in about three months. We had some good times though, going down the Cape to a little town called Cotuit and basking on the beach.

That year, an epidemic of polio broke out in Massachusetts and most of the cases were sent to the Boston hospitals. A floor in Baker Memorial was set aside for the patients, and as soon as you got off the elevator you could hear the "iron lungs" pumping in and out as they forced air into the patients' flaccid lungs. There was a constant smell of axle grease mixed with antiseptic. The patients, who ranged from teens to women up to their thirties, were all pretty calm and relaxed, even though they were encased in these metal and plastic drums with only their heads protruding. It took a little practice to work through the sleeves of the iron lung to give the patient baths and bedpans and I felt slightly uncanny speaking to them through a mirror in front of their faces. In 1955, Dr. Jonas Salk developed the Salk vaccine, which helped many of the cases of the virus. Unfortunately, he did not realize that some of the virus had not been weakened and actually caused the polio. A more effective and safe vaccine, discovered by Dr. Sabin, is used orally today.

While I was dating a boy named Ray, our class was sent to the McLean Hospital in Concord, Massachusetts, for a hands-on experience studying psychology. I had met Ray at one of the MGH student dances, and he started coming to see me in his old jalopy every weekend from the Air Force base on the Cape, where he was stationed.

One Leaf in Time

As luck would have it, I was assigned to Bowditch, the most disturbed patients' cottage. (Why couldn't I have been put in the female ward, a dormitory with three or four nurses on duty at one time?) The male head nurse and I were the only staff on the 7:00 a.m. to 3:00 p.m. shift with seven patients. These patients varied from simple schizophrenics to manic-depressives. One former football star suffered from deep paranoia and was considered quite dangerous. "Don't be caught alone with him," were our orders.

Then there was Hughie, a simple little boy in a huge man's body. He brought out the motherly instincts in me and I loved dressing him and washing his face. We were allowed to walk him to a snack bar to get an ice cream cone. First you had to button up his baggy overalls and comb his hair while he grinned from ear to ear in anticipation. It was such a pleasure to see him enjoying the cone like a five-year-old, rolling his eyes and grinning from one rosy ice-cream-covered cheek to the other. Then back to his room, shuffling along, holding my hand. I wished the patients were all like Hughie!

One morning I was told to escort him to electric therapy on a stretcher. He was strapped down on a table with electrodes attached to his head and several volts of electricity pulsed through his body. His whole frame stiffened and lifted from the table as he clenched his teeth. I wanted to scream, "Stop it!" and pull off the electrodes but in a minute it was over and the poor man slumped lifelessly in a heap. Never would I permit them to do this to a relative of mine, I thought.

Then there was Mr. Mills, a descendant of a famous children's book author residing on Beacon Hill. Mr. Mills was a manic-depressive. He spent the day sitting in a chair with his head bowed down and staring at the floor, smoking.

One day, from the corner of my eye, I saw his lighted cigarette drop down into his shoe. Running over, I quickly bent down to retrieve it. To my surprise, his right fist came up sharply, hitting me in the forehead and almost knocking me out. "I'll never make fast moves around a manic-depressive again," I said to myself.

Among the group was Billy, a young boy interned with a group of men four times his age who were not about to befriend anyone. I felt sorry for him. I had no idea what the approach could be to a psychopathic personality. He looked at me. His vacant blue eyes and tousled, dirty blond hair gave him the look of sixteen years badly spent.

"Want to play ping-pong?" he asked, gesturing at the table placed in the middle of an open sitting area circled with barred-off rooms.

"Sure," I said. "Are you good at ping-pong?"

"I'll go easy on you," he smiled.

"This boy doesn't seem to be mentally ill," I thought. "I wonder why he was put in here?"

One thing led to another until suddenly he suggested I give him a back rub. We went to his room, leaving the barred door open. Suddenly I realized this boy wasn't right. He bragged on about all the girls he had raped behind a haystack in Milford. How they had screamed and tried to get away as he ripped off their clothes and what fun it was. His eyes sparkled and his face lit up with excitement.

"Don't you know what you did was wrong?" was all I could say as I backed out of the doorway.

The next day I was called into the head nurse's office. There sat three of the psychiatrists and the head nurse looking very reproachfully at me.

"Your patient, Bill, tells us that you had sex with him in his room yesterday," they accused me.

"I only gave him a back rub, and his door was open. Everyone could see us," I stammered, and, as usual, tears flooded my eyes as anger welled up inside. What right did they have taking the word of a mental patient over mine? "He wanted to talk and I thought it would help if I gave him a chance to talk out his problems." Finally I convinced them and was released back to work, totally embarrassed and mad.

The next day I was setting the dining room table for their lunch. "Special" silverware was kept in an antique buffet. It consisted mostly of blunt forks and spoons, as their food was served in small pieces.

Turning around with the utensils in hand, I was surprised by several of the patients bursting into the room and pinning my body to the buffet. Evidently Billy was not finished with me. He stood excitedly behind the group chanting, "Get her. Get her!"

"This is a nightmare," I thought, as my knees buckled under me and my body flushed with adrenaline. The men approached with arms outstretched like zombies, eyes glinting and mouths sneering while Billy kept goading them on from the doorway. Then something in me snapped. I made eye contact with each patient and with a trembling voice called each by name and said, "You don't want to do this. Go sit down."

One Leaf in Time

To my amazement, they obeyed, and I heaved a sigh of relief. Perspiration covered my forehead as Billy slunk into a seat with a smug look on his face. He had not won, but he had scared me—that was his purpose.

It was then that I decided psychiatric nursing was not for me, and I was relieved that I had Ray to vent my problems to. Good ole Ray, my boyfriend.

My best experience was in surgery. My roommate and I were assigned to the operating rooms in the Baker Memorial Building. After each operation, the room had to be scrubbed down with phenol and tables and lights made ready for the next patient. We were often asked to scrub in with the various doctors, so we got to see a lot of procedures.

Life in the operating room was never boring. Naturally, we had to memorize all the instruments and stitching material from catgut to Dacron so they could be set up or passed to the surgeon quickly. We never knew what type of surgery or doctor we'd have, either.

One night I was on call for the operating suite. At about 1:00 a.m., the housemother came to our room and knocked on the door. "Miss Churchill, you have an appendectomy coming in to Baker Room 4, get up."

"My gosh," I thought. "I've never even observed an appendectomy!" Throwing on my clothes, I rushed up to the operating suite. As I started my scrub, I turned to see a tall, slender man joining me at the sink. "Hi, I'm Dr. Miller. You must be my scrub nurse." As he spoke, the corners of his steel blue eyes wrinkled up and I could tell there was a huge smile behind his mask.

"I'm afraid I've never assisted in an appendectomy before," I stammered.

"Don't worry," he said firmly, "we'll do fine. Just give me the instruments I call for."

After the first trickle of blood ran down the patient's abdomen from the scalpel's incision, we started to move like a well-oiled machine. Each instrument I handed the doctor went smoothly with a tap into the palm of his hand, handle first. It was amazing to watch Dr. Miller neatly arrange the intestines onto the patient's sterile towel-covered abdomen, explaining each part of the mesentery, blood vessels, and convolutions as he carefully examined the intestines. "There's the culprit!" he exclaimed as he brought the engorged appendix into view. After tying off the appendix and excising it, he cleaned the stem and started to return the man's intestines back to normal. I knew then to change our gloves, discard the first set of instruments, and put my second tray of instruments into use, as the first set of instruments were considered contaminated.

After the stitches were intact and all the sponges counted, Dr. Miller turned to me and, ripping off his mask, gave the grin I had guessed before. It stretched from ear to ear, showing a beautiful row of white teeth in a tender mouth. "Thank you, Miss Churchill," he beamed, shaking my hand. "You were great! Let's go get some sleep."

Of course I had to stay and clean up, but there was a warm glow inside of me as I collected the instruments. "Yes!"

We had just come back from our training in surgery at Baker Memorial when I met Jim Prince. (Ray and I had parted ways when he revealed he was still in love with his old flame. He had driven me to his home in Long Island to meet his mother, but, while there, he kept driving by his old flame's house and talking about the good times they had together.)

As interns, we had just been assigned to Bartlett Hall, a newly built dormitory. It was several stories high with a nice nurses' lounge on the top floor. We all congregated there after our day on the wards, kicking off our shoes and airing our woes.

Walking into Bartlett Hall after work one afternoon, I spied three dejected-looking men sitting in the lobby. It was quite natural for students from other schools to ask us out to dances and social events. (I had dated a boy from MIT but turned him down when he wanted to show me his room.) Anyway, when I approached these three, who looked so much like "hear no evil, see no evil, and speak no evil," they informed me that they were indeed looking for dates to go to a frat party. After I found two of my buddies to join us, I was sorry I didn't ask, "Which frat party?" We ended up at their basement apartment, crawling under hot water pipes and sitting on their cots, drinking "green dragons."

Actually, they behaved quite well and we had several good laughs. One of Jim's roommates made us promise to take off his shirt and hang it up if he got too drunk and fell asleep. "I'm Catholic and I have to wear this shirt to mass tomorrow morning," he said.

All of us returned to the dorm quite sober and I thought, "Well that's that." A few weeks later I received a telephone call. "Sylvia, this is Jim Prince. Do you remember the time we three guys took you over to the apartment and made you green dragons? How would you like to go to the symphony with me on Friday? I just bought the tickets." Gosh, I thought, this guy must be refined and rich. Besides, I kind of liked him. We didn't get invitations to Symphony Hall often.

The evening was great! Jim was quite the gentleman. He was studying to be an optometrist at the Massachusetts College of Optometry and had another year to go. He has never forgiven me for making him leave before the end of the concert though. I had used up my monthly twelve o'clock (which was our curfew hour) and insisted I had to return back to the dorm before I got locked out.

After that, we did a flurry of fun things: enjoying the concerts at the Esplanade, taking in the movie *Carousel* ("If I Loved You" became our song), and going for long walks through the gardens of Boston. Then summer came and Jim was out of school. His father got him a job as a brakeman on the Pennsylvania railroad so he returned to New Jersey to work there again. I missed him so much, but we wrote back and forth each week. I sent him hugs and kisses, and he sent a card with Father Time chasing a blonde nymph. (I guess it pertained to the fact that he was four years older than I.)

Jim popped the question as we were visiting Mom in Manomet. "Are you two going to bed?" Mother's irritated voice came down the hall of her cottage just as Jim was down on one knee proposing to me. We had to laugh. My mother just didn't like people keeping her lights on too late!

CHAPTER 17
A NEW LIFE

To the cadence of "Pomp and Circumstance," on September 1, 1956, we walked in single file down the center aisle of Trinity Church in Boston. Dressed in our starched white uniforms with about twenty-five buttons down each sleeve and our organdy white caps finally circled with a black velvet band, we proudly carried flickering candles. After three full years of training, we were graduating in one of the oldest Episcopal churches in the United States. Her brick-colored turrets and elaborately carved wood pews gave dignity to the ceremony.

September 1956 was a full month for us. On September 15, after Jim had asked Mother for my hand in marriage, we had a wonderful, simple wedding at Christ Church in Plymouth, officiated by Reverend Ernest Pugh.

Jim's dad, Mr. John Prince, took us all out to a lovely rehearsal dinner at a famous lobster restaurant. Jim's cousin was his best man and several of his college buddies were ushers. I asked my three nurse friends to be my bridesmaids and my best friend from high school to be the maid of honor. My little sister, Abigail, made a cute twelve-year-old flower girl dressed in a yellow bouffant lace gown and carrying a basket of daisies.

I had bought my wedding gown for $150 in a little shop under the subway trestle in the North End of Boston. Then I picked out bright, jade green taffeta material for the bridesmaids, who each made her own dress. It was fun, and the girls looked so beautiful in their calf-length, sweetheart-neckline dresses. Tom gave me away.

Mother had the reception at her house, catered by the only African-American member of our church. On Mother's front lawn there were tables set out with wonderful pastries and lobster rolls all prepared by this neat, totally organized, genteel woman. Tom and Harry served guests at an open bar from Mother's basement. Every time one of their Manomet buddies was missing, we knew where they were going!

Dad Prince and I bonded immediately, but Jim's mother was a little reticent. When they came to Boston to meet me for the first time, Mother Prince said, adjusting her veiled, pillbox hat neatly over her immaculate silver coiffure, "So, you want to marry my son!" It had the ring of a policeman apprehending a robber.

"Yes, Jim and I are in love, even though we haven't known each other very long," I replied.

Maybe it was the Asiatic background I had, the fact that I didn't come from a rich family, or just a mother's feeling at the loss of her only child—Mother and I never developed a good rapport, which made me realize what my own mother must have gone through living in Tientsin with her mother-in-law.

After a whirlwind honeymoon at Atlantic Beach, we settled into a second-floor apartment on Revere Street in Boston. Jim was still attending the Massachusetts College of Optometry while I started working on the tenth floor of the White Building of MGH in urology.

The apartment was small, dirty, and had a bed with slats that collapsed every time we turned over. Every window was covered with soot, and even after I scrubbed them, the floors were black from dirt, not paint as I had assumed.

Shortly after we moved in, Jim took me to the closet and said, "I want you to check my clothes each week. Sew on any loose buttons and mend any holes in my pockets." This started our first marital discordance. While he was in the Navy, he was used to having his uniform cleaned and pressed by an orderly and his shoes were always spit-shined.

The blood flowed up to my head and my cheeks turned red as I clenched my fists and looked at him in disbelief. My father was able to have his clothes cleaned and pressed by servants when he lived in Tientsin. Was I supposed to be Jim's servant?!

"If you want something mended you bring it to me. I'll do it when I can," I screamed. Then I ran, tears streaming, into the bedroom, slamming the door behind me. He never brought up the subject again, but it gave me a sinking feeling as I realized that marriage was not always a bed of roses.

After that first spat, we got into a good routine: Jim would go to the College of Optometry in the mornings for his classes while I slept late, waking up at nine. I'd clean the apartment, fix him a meal at 2:00 p.m. (leaving it on the stove), then walk down the three blocks to Massachusetts General Hospital where I worked the relief shift on White 10. At midnight, Jim picked me up from the hospital and we walked back up the hill, sometimes having to step over tea bags, scrambled eggs, and old tin cans. Occasionally I had the 7:00 a.m. to 3:00 p.m. shift.

I loved working on the urology floor. Most of the patients were little old Italian men who had TURS (transurethral resections) for enlarged prostates. They enjoyed our attention and the camaraderie with the other patients in their four-bed units. Sitting by their beds, attached to five-gallon jugs by way of Foley catheters, they cracked jokes and told stories. It was a happy floor most of the time. Medicines were not difficult to learn either, as there were few heart medications or antibiotics discovered at the time. Laxatives, antacids, and pain medicines were prescribed most often, and we passed them out arranged on a tray, in little paper cups.

At ten o'clock, when I was on the 3:00 to 11:00 p.m. or relief shift, I had to collect all the five-gallon jugs on a metal cart and measure and empty them in the utility room. The smell of urine was not very pleasant, and the large glass jugs were extremely heavy, but it facilitated a chance to check for bleeding and amount of output, which we charted in the Kardex.

One night, while I was on the relief shift, a restless patient caught my attention as I was doing rounds. We had about forty patients, so it was hard to give each one a lot of attention; therefore, we made rounds to determine each patient's condition. He was in a lot of pain but did not have a medication order. There was a medical student on call in a small room on the floor. I hurried to the room and knocked on the door. There was no answer. I knocked again. Still no answer, so I opened the door, thinking I would awaken the sleeping doctor. To my surprise, the med student sprung from the couch in a furor. There, neatly hung on the back of a chair, were his trousers. He probably hung them there to keep them from creasing. "I need a pain med order for Mr. Feruchi," I stammered, but it did not calm him. "How dare you walk in the room on me without knocking?" he scolded. I made my apologies and backed out. It was bizarre that I had forty men running around in scant "johnnies" and he was so upset at my seeing him in a pair of shorts.

The next day, I was put on the morning shift and was making beds when the doctors came on rounds. The house doctor had a trail of Harvard medical students following behind him and one of them was my infamous medical student. Stopping at the bed I was making, the house doctor said with a big grin, "Are you the nurse that caught my medical student with his pants down?" A snicker and then laughter broke loose from the students while my medical student, with crimson face, tried to hide behind the others. All I could do was gulp and whisper "Yes, sir" with my head bent down.

I couldn't wait to tell Jim the good news. Bursting into the apartment, I breathlessly sputtered, "Jim, I'm pregnant!"

"You can't be, it's not practical," he gasped.

We had tried several types of contraceptives, but none worked. Unfortunately, the pill was not in existence at that time, and other methods were hit or miss.

"Well, practical or not, I'm having our baby," I snorted, my balloon deflated.

"Oh, Sylvia," Mother's voice rang loud and clear over the phone. She rarely called, so I knew she had important news. There was excitement in her voice as she said, "I've decided to visit England with the money I saved and see my mother. She's not in good health, you know, and they have her in a nursing home, a good one mind you, but if I don't do this now, she may be gone." Grandmother, Mary Westgarth, was in her eighties and becoming quite senile. Mother had not seen her in a long time.

"I'm taking your sister with me. Tom and Harry are helping me pay for the transatlantic ship, and we will be gone for several weeks. Sorry, I won't be there when you have the baby though."

What a time for her to leave me, six months pregnant and starting into the summer heat of Boston. She had it all planned: my cousin Brian was to meet her and take her and Gail on a tour of London and visits to all the kinsfolk—her sister and brother-in-law, Dolly and Arthur Sharp in Yorkshire, Mother's sister-in-law Connie in Hartlepool, her sister's children, Arthur and Vera, in Yorkshire, then back to Hartlepool to visit Brian's wife, Freda, and their son, Ian. While in London they stopped to visit John and Cissy; John worked at the BBC and was Mother's nephew. Then at last she would visit with her mother in the nursing home at Seaton Carew.

"I hate just leaving the boys all that time." Tom and Harry were not married in 1956, and they were desperately trying to keep Dad's Esso gas station business afloat while Tom was attending Northeastern University in Boston as well.

"There is no reason for me to stay in Boston, Mother," I told her. "I have taken a leave of absence from MGH and Jim is busy with his last year of optometry school and can live in with a few of his school chums who have an apartment. I'll come down to the Cape, watch the house, and take care of my brothers."

There was never a more stupid statement uttered. As soon as Mother and Gail tootled off to England, I settled down in her flat-roofed cottage in Manomet. It would be like a vacation, I told myself. The beach wasn't far away, and I could stretch out on Mother's lawn chair, away from the sooty city, in her front yard. That was the good side . . .

In the heat of her non-air-conditioned home, there were overalls and shirts to iron. The gas station required clean, pressed overall uniforms with the boys' names embroidered on them, and Jim dressed in button-down shirts, which he brought down each weekend for me to launder.

To add to the fun, it was hard to find menus to satisfy both brothers' palettes. If I made a beef stew or even a roast, Harry would say, "Nah, just give me some eggs," while Tom would smack his lips. If I just scrambled some eggs, Tom would look hurt and Harry was happy. Harry could eat a whole egg, in the shell, raw.

Jim came down on the weekends and brought meat and vegetables he had picked up in Scully Square. Groceries came to the end of the line in Boston, on the train. Produce was cheaper, but you had to be careful you were not obtaining spoiled goods, or that the grocer wasn't weighing with his thumb on the scale. One time Jim arrived with a slimy, gray piece of liver. Blood was oozing out of all the protruding veins and I lost it! "Take this away, I don't want to look at it and I can't eat it," I cried.

One Leaf in Time

I woke up on August 12, 1956, with clear fluid dripping from me. The baby wasn't supposed to be born for another four weeks, so the first thing that struck me was that I had a urinary tract infection. The day before, I had climbed up and down the 150 steps to the beach and was pretty exhausted. Could that be it?

Mother's friend, Margaret, lived just down the path, so I walked over to ask her advice. "Get in the car, Sylvia," she said, "I'm no rabbit catcher!"

Sitting on a towel, I drove to Boston with Margaret as copilot to show me the way—first to the apartment where Jim had been staying, then when his roommate, Todd, started to get nervous and pale, to the Boston Lying-In Hospital where I was scheduled to deliver. Jim, meanwhile, had stayed over at the college to move chairs. It was scary enough not to have your mate at your side, but the obstetrician on call came into the room with a tale of gloom. Sitting on the side of my bed, he proceeded to tell me the baby was too early, and with the membranes ruptured since morning, the baby would be infected. Just then Jim appeared at the elevator door. They would not let him step a foot into the hall, but he gave me a kiss as they wheeled me by the elevator door on my way to the delivery room. How different it is now when the fathers are encouraged to stay with the mother and even cut the baby's cord.

I had practiced Lamaze (a form of natural childbirth), but under such strain, it all went out the window and I almost suffocated an Asian medical student as the hospital staff were trying to give me spinal anesthesia. The anesthetist even broke the needle in my spine. Poor John Bowman struggled into the world a five-and-a-half-pound preemie and was rushed to the neonatal care unit before I even got a chance to hold him. He thrived and did well there, although I could only view him through a glass window for several weeks.

Notice published in the Tientsin Daily News dated 1st, January 1953.

Notice
by

The Tientsin Peoples Government
House and Land Control Bureau

Owing to illness, Tso-Law-Shih passed away on 30th August 1952. The deceased left property consisting of one House including Furniture and Sundry articles (wearing apparel etc.), situated at Wu Chia Ta Yao Street, No.40, and also cash. Since no legal heir is here to inherit this property, the Peoples Government has decided to keep said property in custody for the period of one year, as from 31st August 1952 to August 30th 1953. During this period if no legal heir claims the said property, the Peoples Government will dispose of same as it will deem fit.

Whereby this is brought to public notice.

December 30th, 1952.

Translation of document my father received telling him of my grandmother's death in China in 1952

Mom with Abigail

Dad at his Esso Gas Station in Kingston

Cleaning up in the Baker Operating Room

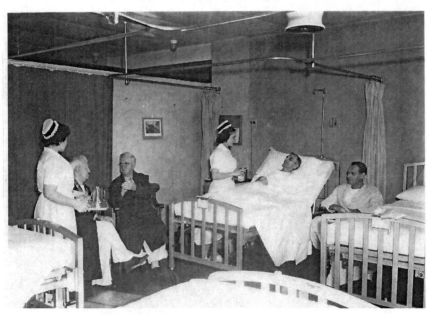

Four-bed unit at Massachusetts General Hospital. I am in the center.

Ensign James Prince, U.S. Navy

Graduate of Massachusetts General
Hospital School of Nursing

We were married in September, 1956.

Mary, Midge, Sue, and John at Eastertime, 1965

The Apollo Camper

CHAPTER 18
MORE RABBITS

After Jim graduated from Massachusetts College of Optometry, we moved to Richmond, Virginia. It was a bittersweet experience, as I wanted to go and start a new life with my husband, but at the same time hated having to leave my mother and siblings.

"Can't we take Johnny with us?" I pleaded.

"No, it would be too difficult to look for a house and get settled with a baby on our hands," Jim reasoned.

So it was that I had to leave my first-born, preemie baby with Jim's parents for a month. I was fearful that Jim's mother, who was in her seventies, would not be capable of caring for such a young child, but reluctantly, I gave in.

It turned out for the best. Jim started working with Dr. Marvin Rightmiller in Richmond immediately, and for several days we slept on the floor in the little cracker-box house that we found. Our total possessions consisted of an Oriental carpet my mother had given us, a card table that we ate off of, and an old Singer sewing machine that I bought myself while I was a student nurse. Mother and Dad Prince brought Johnny down from their home in New Jersey in their big gray Buick. In those days, there were no car seats for children so they laid him between them on the front seat. To Dad's amusement, the gas station attendant kept looking at this elderly couple and then at the baby as he cleaned the windshield. Finally, Dad whispered in the attendant's ear, "I'll give you the name of the place I get my pills from for a price!" Today it would not be that unusual with all the medicines and procedures like artificial insemination and the attendant would probably have shrugged his shoulders and thought, "Good luck!"

We did get a nice mahogany bedroom set and kitchen table eventually, but the two years we spent on Monument Avenue were cramped and cold. I became good friends with a young soldier's wife next door. She had three small children. How they fit in that small house I don't know. I marveled at her Southern accent. At first I couldn't understand her "cutting" the lights and TV on and off and "Say what?" but she always had a big grin on her face and a story to tell me about her kids that would make me laugh. From her, I obtained a chest of drawers and a baby high chair that I used for all my children. She didn't mind that her husband was stationed in Norfolk and she only saw him on weekends. "Hell, I can do what I like, eat what I want and watch my own TV" was her motto.

My other neighbor would hang her wash out at the same time as I did and we soon got to be good friends. In fact, we still correspond though we are miles apart now.

By 1958, I found I was pregnant again. We moved to a larger home in Lakeside, and I was thrilled that the elementary school was located right across the street so Johnny could start school there. We also enjoyed the large backyard and often I would take Johnny and Susan, after she was born, to the train tracks to wave at the engineer of the train. It was about a two-mile walk but worth it to see Johnny so excited as the engineer of the train would wave and "toot" the horn at him. We had only one car so I had to push the baby carriage, in the other direction, about four blocks, to buy groceries.

It was a stormy night when Sue decided to make her entrance into the world. Thank goodness Jim was home and my little sister, Gail, had come to visit for a week.

"Jim, wake up," I said as I shook him.

"Are you sure you're having contractions?" was his sleepy reply. "You aren't due for two more weeks and it's raining and nasty outside."

"Yes, I've been timing them since midnight and they are every three minutes now."

Quickly we awakened my poor, confused teenage sister, who happened to be visiting, and threw some clothes into a suitcase. The storm had gotten worse. Strong winds were blowing tree limbs across the roads and wind and rain splashed against the windshield as Jim picked his way through Richmond to Richmond Memorial Hospital. By the wee hours of the morning on July 1, 1959, Susan Mae Prince was born. I wanted to call her Virginia Gail, but Jim felt that was too corny and Susan was his grandmother's name. Susan Mae it was, and even Gail, who had stayed behind to take care of Johnny, was left out.

One Leaf in Time

Jim started driving to a little town called Kilmarnock, where Dr. Rightmiller had a satellite practice, so I was left without a car all week. The Richmond office on Franklin Street was too far for Jim to walk. He stayed at that office until Friday, then drove to Kilmarnock until Sunday night.

I was very lonely at Lakeside. With Jim gone three days of the week and two young children to care for, postpartum depression descended. (I say "descended" because it comes like a cloud and wraps around you.) I'd get all energized and start cleaning the venetian blinds, and, halfway through, I'd sit down in a lump on the floor, crying my eyes out.

"Ask Doctor Cotts what you can take," Jim suggested. The great doctor put me on Dexedrine. It only made me nervous and shaky, so I tabled that and eventually got over the depression anyway.

When we bought the house on Cottage Street in Lakeside, we didn't realize it was in a flood plain. One weekend, while Jim was in Kilmarnock, the heavens opened and we were deluged by rain. I woke up to find water up to our windowsills and the furnace, which was under the house, not working. There was no electricity so I couldn't even warm a baby bottle. Sue, who had been fighting a bout of colic, was screaming, and poor little John sat shivering in a corner.

"You've got to come home and help us!" I telephoned Jim. (The same feeling must have terrorized the people of New Orleans during Hurricane Katrina.) I couldn't get out, and everyone around us was in the same boat, so no one could come in to save us. Eventually the river of water receded and Jim called the furnace people to repair our furnace. "We're sorry, but your furnace will have to be replaced," they told us. "It will take about two weeks, so you had best find someplace to send your family."

Jim looked at me all bundled up with the baby close to my body and said, "I'm going to call my folks up in New Jersey and send you and the kids up to them on the train." I didn't want to go, as Mother Prince always made me feel uncomfortable, but I knew it would be impossible to stay in that cold house with a baby and a two-year-old. There just wasn't enough money for us to rent an apartment or stay at a motel.

So I packed what I could carry and Jim drove us to the station. Dad and Mother Prince said they would be happy to have us stay, but the trip was horrific, as Susan cried and messed diapers all the way up, and poor little John, confused and disoriented, held tightly to my slacks through the whole journey.

Jim, meanwhile, bought a huge packet of split peas and, with a ham bone I'd left in the refrigerator, ate pea soup the whole time, climbing into an igloo he'd made out of a pile of blankets to sleep. When I returned back home, there were dried peas all over the kitchen.

Mother Prince got sick of Susan's crying. It was constant and neither of us could get any sleep. We tried everything: rocking, walking with her, and even putting her facedown in a quiet room and letting her cry. Finally Mother said, "Catnip and fennel. My mother swore by it." I thought she was going to poison my baby, but to my surprise in just a few days the catnip tea worked and Sue settled down to a quieter rest. I learned the hard way, "Mother knows best."

By 1960, we were moving again. Dr. R. had developed multiple sclerosis and could not drive, so we opted to take the Kilmarnock office. Jim would then have his own practice and not such a distance to drive.

I had mixed feelings. We would have to leave the neighborhood where John was about to go to school, and for the third time I was pregnant! We packed what meager belongings we had—most of our living room furniture came from Green Stamps, which were given out as an incentive by grocery stores, and if you got enough pasted in your books, you could purchase sundry items—and piled the kids into the old Plymouth. Crossing the Rappahannock River on the newly built Norris Bridge, my spirits were lifted. After all, this seemed like a small, friendly community similar to Manomet. Not!

If you were not born in the Northern Neck, you were a "come here." You could not participate in the local gossip as you were ignorant as to whose mother was whose sister or what family that child came from. Furthermore, there were inklings that the foreigners were corrupting and taking over the Northern Neck, so you became a sort of enemy. However, the colors of springtime with pure-white dogwood and pink, red, and purple azaleas soon won me over. Every time we cross the azure Rappahannock River now, I know we are coming home. After living here for fifty-four years, we are almost not "come heres."

We tried to fit into the community, but it was hard. Jim would go into town every night and sit at the Main Street drugstore counter and try to make himself "known," and on Sundays he played golf with a friend from Irvington, which left me with the children almost all of the time. We even tried to have a party and invite neighbors in, but the only response I got was having a neighbor call me to ask for Jim's clam dip recipe, as she was having a party to which we were not invited.

Marjorie Ann came on October 15, 1960, after a bumpy ride over the Tappahannock Bridge. With each bump, I had another contraction. "Hurry up," I said to Jim, "unless you want to deliver this baby!" By the time I reached Richmond Memorial, however, the contractions had stopped and I sat for hours, wondering where Doctor Cotts was.

"Sorry I'm late," he said jovially when he arrived. "I had to deliver my horse first. Although you're awfully early, I'll give you something and we'll get you started."

The nurse came in with a syringe full of what must have been Pitocin and injected it into the IV line. Away I went! First I saw black spots, then stars, and then tremendous contractions racked my body. In just half an hour of tremendous pain, my four-and-a-half-pound baby girl was delivered. "I don't want to deliver this way again," I thought.

That night, Jim didn't dare go home because the neighbors would think something was going on between him and his secretary, who had kindly agreed to stay at the house with the two other children. He opted to sleep in his car instead.

Marjorie turned out to be the quietest child I had. She often lay bundled up on the couch while the other two tickled her feet and played around her. It didn't take long for her to gain weight, but she remained short, so we called her Midge.

Midge was only ten months old when I found I was pregnant again! It was hot and dismal in the little brick house on Roseneath Avenue and as August drew near, I became more and more despondent.

Where Midge was small and quiet with big brown sober eyes and jet-black hair, Mary was chubby, active, and bald! Born on August 23, 1961, she weighed seven pounds, six ounces. Mary Elizabeth was to sleep in her playpen for a year because "there was no room in the inn," so to speak. The walls of our small second bedroom were lined with various baby beds.

She learned to crawl early, possibly because she had to keep up with her siblings. One night, as I was serving dinner to the crew, Mary was left to play on the floor in the living room.

"Where's Mary?" Sue asked when it seemed too quiet in the living room. Going to check, I found my seven-month-old daughter sitting in the bathroom with an array of pills spread around her. Red, green, and white pills spilled out on the floor from an old cigar box we used as our medicine cabinet. From her mouth oozed green and pink drool.

"Help me," I yelled, "Mary's gotten into a bunch of medicines and my Dexedrine was in there!"

"Oh," said Johnny, "I took the box down from the top shelf to get a Band-Aid."

We rushed her to Doctor Gravatt's clinic and with his usual calm he pumped out the poor child's stomach. It was far from calm all that night, however. The Dexedrine had taken effect and Mary was on her feet trying to walk all night long. I had to hold her hands and walk with her until morning, when we both dropped from exhaustion.

Susan was always putting things into her mouth also. One time when she was a baby, we were visiting Jim's parents at Christmas and she managed to crawl into Mother's clothes closet and devour half a mothball. We rushed her to the nearest hospital emergency room in Union, New Jersey, where the doctor shook his head and said, "If it had been a whole mothball, she may be in trouble, but just a half of one— she'll be okay."

Being the older brother, Johnny was always proud of his harem of sisters, and on one occasion, when he was four, he hailed a neighbor passing by and said, "Let me introduce you to my sister Sue." With that, he foraged under a forsythia bush, dusted her off and proudly produced a curly-haired two-year-old with berry juice drooling from her mouth. The neighbor was so amused he had to tell me about it.

"You should get the children baptized," my mother said. So we arranged it with the Grace Church minister and Mom came down from Manomet in the Greyhound bus at one o'clock in the morning. Jim had to go to Warsaw to pick her up. She was a trouper. It was so comforting to have my mother by my side for a week. We enjoyed cups of tea together and trips across the Merry Point ferry to get apples from a local farm.

John F. Kennedy was sworn in as president just about the time Jim decided we needed to invest in a home that would hold our burgeoning family. After much debate and discussion, we settled for a redwood home built on a small piece of cornfield at the edge of Kilmarnock. It was like a dream come true, with three bedrooms, two baths, and a large ground-entrance basement.

One Leaf in Time

The afternoon of November 22, 1963, started out like any other, waiting for the children to get up from their naps. We had just moved into our ranch-style home at Walnut Court and I was in pig heaven. Finally, we had enough bedrooms and a basement that the children used as their playroom. Barbie dolls and bikes littered the back, while a workbench carried Jim's tools and later the children's science projects.

Usually, I was not one to turn on the TV in the afternoon, but President Kennedy was driving through Dallas, Texas, and the first lady was with him in the motorcade. Jacqueline Kennedy was noted for her beautiful suits. I just had to check it out.

President Kennedy suffered the whole time he was in office. Though it was not made public, he was diagnosed with Addison's disease. Just like Dad. His lower spine gave him a lot of pain, forcing him to use crutches occasionally. When he was speaking in public, he would use his brother Bobby's arm for support. Everyone knew he had a special rocking chair he loved to sit in.

There they were, riding in an open convertible with secret servicemen walking beside and behind it. As they waved to the crowds along the street, Jacqueline was radiant in her pink pillbox hat and matching pink wool suit accented with large buttons and a pearl necklace. John Kennedy's well-tanned face was highlighted by his broad, toothy grin. They looked so regal.

It wasn't to last. Just as the motorcade passed the Book Depository building in downtown Dallas, two cracks rang out. At first I thought someone had set off firecrackers, but the announcer was saying, "Wait a minute, I think the president's been shot!" Like seeing a horror movie, I watched as one of the secret servicemen jumped over the back of the convertible to cover the slumped body of the president. Jacqueline, with his head in her lap, had blood splattered all over that pink suit. It happened so fast; and then the limousine sped away.

I had to blink my eyes to make sure it wasn't a crazy dream or some sort of bizarre ritual. The screams and melee that followed convinced me it wasn't. (What a feeling of loss and despair.) Even the news commentator's voice cracked; on the verge of tears, he announced that John F. Kennedy died of a bullet wound to the head shortly after he was taken to the hospital.

Sixty, seventy, eighty! The car bolted ahead as I jammed my foot on the accelerator. Staying in the house alone with four children for five years had gotten to me. Tears rolled down my face as I gripped the steering wheel and sped down Irvington Road. It wasn't fair. After studying for three solid years at a fine hospital, I couldn't fulfill my dreams. Here I was in a hick town with children and demeaning housework! Now I was at ninety and creeping up to one hundred miles an hour. Between sobs, a song on the radio broke into my cognizance. "Stand by me, oh stand by me—" It was so pertinent, as if Jim were speaking to me; it broke into my orgy of self-pity.

After all, I loved Jim and the children and wouldn't exchange a one (actually I had said I wanted a dozen). Did I not say in the marriage vows that I would cherish, honor, and obey? As Robert Frost wrote in *The Road Not Taken*, "Two roads diverged in a yellow wood, and sorry I could not travel both . . . " The path you pick always leaves you thinking, "What if?"

However, Betty Friedan wrote in *The Feminine Mystique* that a woman should not feel it was her obligation to have a husband and children, but should be able to "aspire to separate identities as individuals." Her book was very popular in the 1960s. In 1984, less than thirty years after Friedan's book came out, a woman was nominated for vice-president.

My foot lifted off the accelerator. Pulling to the side of the road, I burst into a cathartic flood of tears. "The kids will be home from school," I thought, drying my tears, so I headed back to the house. It is also strange, that a woman instinctively thinks of the whereabouts of her children while a man can kiss his wife goodbye and head to work without a thought about his children all day.

Before Tom was born, two angels came to my aid. The first was a Baptist minister, John Houghton, who had heard that Jim was Baptist, and came to invite us to the Kilmarnock Baptist Church. He was a soft-spoken, broad-shouldered, stocky man with penetrating brown eyes and a close-shaven head.

"Hello, Sylvia, I'm the minister of the Baptist church here in town. How are you doing?" It had been a trying day with children whining, spilling food, and demanding my attention constantly. Jim had gone into town right after supper to his usual perch at the soda fountain in the Main Street drug store in order to be "seen" by possible patients.

Without thinking, I threw myself into the arms of this sympathetic stranger and started to cry. To my astonishment, he let me blubber on his shoulder, like a child with a new hurt. "There, there," he consoled me as he patted me on the back. "What's wrong?" He seemed to know how lonely I was.

"I'm so embarrassed," I mumbled, sopping my tears off on his T-shirt.

"Don't think anything of it!" he smiled. "You know you should get out a bit, Sylvia, get away from the kids for a while. If you want to continue in the Episcopal Church, there is one just at the end of this road. Of course you'll always be welcome at the Baptists. We have a lot of good folks, you know." We talked for a while and I felt so much better. It was a weight lifted off my shoulders. Someone cared that I existed!

Shortly after that I became a member of Grace Episcopal Church and took all four children, dressed and shined, each Sunday. Jim decided that it would be best that we both belonged to one church, so on February 10, 1966, he went through confirmation classes and became a member, too. It felt so good to go to church as a family.

The second angel was a longtime member of Grace. Kaggy's grandmother lived next door to us and, after visiting her one day, Kaggy Chase knocked at my door. "Sylvia, would you like to join the Women's Club? I'd like to sponsor you. We meet just once a month." It was like manna from heaven. A place to go dressed up, with people to talk to without the children!

It was at one of these meetings that a retired general was speaking about his tour in China after World War II. The room was packed with members when General Black started to talk about the Communists and his experiences in China in 1945. He had travelled all over China, but suddenly I realized he was referring to his assignment in Tientsin and how cruel the Communists actually were. This being my hometown, I immediately started paying more attention. "Yes, as an example," General Black was saying, "not only did the people have no freedom of speech, they were only allowed one child per couple and had to adhere to the doctrines of Mao and his 'little red book.' But the youth were so brainwashed that a young girl, believing so strongly in the doctrines, reported her own father to the police. Chung Mei, a wealthy, industrious carpet manufacturer, was then beheaded because of his beliefs."

"Chung Mei!" The name resounded in my head. Quickly I drove home and turned over a sample of carpet Dad had given me. The small oval rug was in disrepair after accompanying the girls to college, but there along the burlap-bound edge in bold black lettering was stamped "Chung Mei Carpet Company." Dad worked for this company from 1925 to 1934. So that's what had happened to poor Mr. Chung Mei! All the years that Dad had tried to contact the man and never knew his fate. It gave me an eerie feeling. He had even received a shipment of carpets from Mr. Mei, but when Dad wrote back for instructions about price and payments, the letters were returned. The whole warehouse full of carpets was confiscated because Dad didn't have the money for their storage and shipping.

CHAPTER 19
INTO THE SUNSHINE

By 1972 we had bought a little Aristocrat motor home. It had a large bed over the cab, a table that lowered into a bed, and a couch that formed a double bed—all in a twenty-one-foot space. The part that tickled me was the small bathroom that was wallpapered with outhouses and people hanging out of them. Actually, this was quite realistic, as whoever was on the throne would be hurled into the washbasin or against the door whenever Jim applied the brakes or rounded a corner.

The best trip we took was to Quebec and Percé, Nova Scotia. The roads were lined with small cottages, each with window boxes filled with flowers. As we approached Perce, the roads became very narrow and rough. Some were even unpaved. When we stopped, we saw that a tomato I had placed on the shelf of the refrigerator had been grated right through the rack.

Finally, we found a campground. "I need a drink," sighed Jim. "Sioux" (Sue had changed her name because of Jim's Cherokee ancestors), "you just had French in school. Go ask the camp manager where the nearest liquor store is."

"I can't do that!" gasped Sioux. "Mrs. Hill never taught us that kind of French."

After the camp manager heard our problem, he died laughing. "*Ou est Le Commission de Liquor, Susie,*" he kept shouting from his doorway.

The Gaspé Peninsula was very primitive, with mud ovens built in front of each home, from which the French Canadians baked the most delicious breads, and fishing villages with codfish drying in the sun on racks. We really enjoyed hiking and visiting the pristine towns.

While we bumped along, the girls sang:

When I was an itty, bitty boy . . .
We'd go down to Grandma's house . . .
And sleep in her feather bed.
It was nine feet tall and six feet wide—
Soft as a downy chick.
It was made from the feathers of forty-'leven geese,
Took a whole bolt of cloth for the tick.
It'd hold eight kids and four hound dogs
And a piggy we stole from the shed.
We didn't get much sleep
But we had a lot of fun
In Grandma's featherbed.

They sang it so fast that I couldn't keep up with them, but I usually joined in when it came to "a piggy we stole from the shed." Then we would all start laughing.

John Denver's songs were terrifically popular just as the kids were going into their teens, so we serenaded Jim, who had an American Optometric Association meeting in Houston, Texas. We took the motor home and all four kids and started traveling down Route 41, singing lustily.

As we drove through Arkansas, Sioux was turning thirteen and the only thing she wanted for her birthday was a dulcimer. When we reached Dog Patch, there were Little Abner and Daisy Mae painted on a huge shed and close by a country store loaded with all sorts of dulcimers. The rest of the trip was spent with Sioux twanging on her dulcimer and all of us singing "Country Roads," "Matthew," and whatever words we could remember of Denver's songs. We were pretty hoarse by the time we reached the hotel.

After the convention closed, Jim headed the Aristocrat farther southwest, visiting the Alamo in Texas, Judge Roy Bean's cabin, where the judge had presided as the only law west of the Mississippi, and Carlsbad Caverns in the Guadalupe Mountains of New Mexico. At the caverns, we stopped to do our laundry. John was sitting on a pile of logs by the laundry room door when an old Westerner muttered, "Get up quick!" and grabbed John's arm. There, sitting on the log next to him was, a large scorpion!

That night we waited for the bats to leave this huge cave. It was a balmy evening as we sat in anticipation on the hillside. There must have been one hundred people waiting for this great event. As the sun set and dusk settled around the cave, we started to hear a fluttering, whirring sound. Then, all of a sudden, like a cannonball bursting out of a cannon, the bats emerged in a black swarm, emitting high-pitched squeaks and flying up into the air, where they parted and spread out to their own territories of the night. It was amazing and happened so fast that one was left thinking, "Did I really see that?" We had so many good memories from that trip.

"The camper is getting too cramped, Sylvia, and I'd feel safer with double wheels under us," Jim said one morning. "I see where they are having a big camper show up in Washington this weekend. Would you like to go?"

"Great!" I said. The children loved to go on trips to Washington to browse through the Smithsonian and visit the zoo. We would stay at a Marriott Hotel at the edge of town and take the subway in early in the morning.

The year before, we had gone to Cape Hatteras in the Aristocrat, promising my mother a wonderful time. A large storm hit the coast just as we got there. Jim could hardly control the little motor home as we crossed the Bay Bridge. Poor Mom, we scared her to death with Jim shouting, "Sylvia, I can't control the camper. It is being pushed over by the wind and I can't see through the sheets of rain!" We managed to make it across, but while the kids were wrestling and arguing in the back, Mom sat pale as a ghost. That night, she had to sleep in a motel, where the beds were dampened by the rain, because of lack of space in our little camper. She was madder than a wet hen when we picked her up the next morning.

So we traded the Aristocrat for an Apollo motor home. "It's just like the one that Bob Hope lives in when he is parked at a movie set," the salesman said—I was impressed. (Also, the fact that there were six big drawers, a huge bed, and a lovely bath with lighted mirrors in the bathroom made it more desirable.)

The American Optometric Association convention was in San Francisco in 1973, so Jim planned a six-week trip for our summer vacation. It was tremendous! He had found a young optometrist, who was eager to get a taste of the Northern Neck to cover the practice. So we loaded up the Apollo with cans of fruit, vegetables, tuna fish, and bedding. The three girls just fit on the back bed, the two boys on the overhead bunk, and Jim and I on the drop-down dining table.

Our goal was to visit twelve reserves and national parks. Hiking along the crumbling paths of sandstone with the rusty red and yellow precipices at Zion National Park and over the windblown mesas of Bandelier, we wound our way from the Alamo to Taos, New Mexico.

At Bandelier, we marveled at the ingenuity of the prehistoric cliff dwellers. They had built communal homes high up in the side of the rock cliffs with irrigation and fire pits in the caves. I thought at the time, "These Indians must have been in good shape to climb up the sixty- to eighty-foot stick ladders to their secure homes."

From Santa Fe, New Mexico, Jim steered the motor home up through Arizona and stopped at the Petrified Forest National Park. Trees that had grown 225 million years ago had been buried with mud, sand, and volcanic ash and had turned into stone. Each piece showed the minute detail of the tree, such as the different colorations of the swirls inside the trunk. Six forests are within the park, which covers 95,000 acres, but the prettiest is called Rainbow Forest. It was hard for us to keep the kids from climbing and playing hide-and-seek behind these large fragmented fossils. Of course they had to have souvenirs of the stone from the gift shop. "What changes in time these ancient polished stones have seen," I said to the children.

Back in the Apollo we headed towards the Grand Canyon. First we stopped at Bryce Canyon with its beautiful wind-carved shapes and colorful rock formations, and then to the Grand Canyon! The Colorado River wound along the bottom, looking like a blue ribbon lying between miles of purple, gold, and bronze walls with a large ship-shaped island, sitting like a monument, in the center. Clusters of pinion pine and sagebrush clutched to the walls and stood along the floor of this gigantic crevice. It was so beautiful it was unreal, making you inhale in amazement. People of all ages and types were attempting to hike down the trail, but the most comical was a middle-aged lady dressed to the hilt in coordinated Western gear stepping gingerly on each mule plop with her shiny leather Western boots. "I know the mules and donkeys know the safest route on this trail so I'm following their tracks," she grinned, tipping her cowboy hat.

"I've made reservations to go down the Kaibab Trail to the Gardens," Jim told us, pulling out the map they had given us at the ranger station. "It's about two miles long but very steep, so we'll need to wear our hiking boots and protective gear." I looked at my brand-new boots. They were very stiff and awkward, so I hadn't worn them at the other stops, but this time I should, I thought.

We started early the next morning. The sun was just rising over the farthest rim of the canyon, sending shafts of light onto the yellow, copper and gold walls. Chipmunks and squirrels scurried about looking for nuts and a Steller's jay chattered from a tree. Dressed in overalls, flannel shirts, and straw hats, we started down the dusty, dung-strewn trail. The dung had a musty smell and where there were fresh droppings a little wisp of steam would rise from its warmth.

The trail was so steep that our toes kept stubbing into the front of our boots and I soon realized that it was a bad mistake to wear new ones on such a trek. My feet kept sliding back and forth until a huge blister formed on the ball of my right foot. "I can't go any farther," I complained.

"It's only another mile," Jim said. "You can soak your foot in the river when we get there. Besides, it costs a lot of money to have a helicopter come down to pick you up."

I was so happy to finally see the gardens and the Colorado River. The blister, which had gotten as large as a tennis ball, had burst; soaking it in the ice-cold river water with small trout nibbling at my toes perked up my spirits. A wonderful dinner was served at the main cabin and the seven of us settled into another cabin for the night—but not for long.

"Something is scratching inside the ceiling over my head," announced Midge.

"There is a squirrel inside our bag of peanut butter nabs and he's eating them all up," called Johnny from the screened porch where he was sleeping.

Sure enough, the critters had taken over! There were mice all over the cabin, so we sent John over to ask for a mousetrap. He appeared five minutes later with a big rattrap. "Oh, well, I'll just bait it with a peanut butter nab and it might catch one," sighed Jim. We had just closed the lights again when we heard a loud "munch, munch" from the trap. Switching on the light, Jim expected he had caught a large rodent but instead, a cute little mouse with huge pink ears sat calmly eating away in the middle of the rattrap. That night, none of us got much sleep. The mice ruled.

The next morning, we dressed back into our dusty jeans and after a sumptuous breakfast climbed regrettably out of the Grand Canyon on the

Bright Angel trail. I had found a long stick that I used as a crutch but each step was agony. The memory of that fabulous experience, however, made it well worth it.

Back on the road again, Jim headed for Sequoia National Park in California. "Look, Mom," chimed Sioux, "there's a roadside stand. Let's stop and get those beautiful cherries!"

They were the biggest cherries I have ever seen; we bought a box and popped them into the refrigerator. "We'll have them when we stop for breakfast," I told the kids. Little did we know that California had quarantined produce grown outside of its borders. As soon as we reached the California line, we were stopped.

"Let me see what you have in the refrig," the border guard said as he whipped open its door. "Aha, cherries! You can't take these into the state."

Before I could pass the beautiful fruit out to the children to eat on the spot, he was out the door of the Apollo cuddling the forbidden fruit to his chest. "Well darn!" the kids chorused dejectedly.

Sequoia was beautiful—not in the same way as the other parks but in an earthy, almost religious feeling of grandeur. The sequoia trees stood immensely tall over our heads, reaching as if to touch the sky, while the odor from their needles was heady and fresh. All the area around was carpeted with needles and the campsites were interspersed between these stately ancient sentinels.

That night we awoke to a crash, bang, clatter! A great big grizzly bear had decided to raid the garbage cans. As he worked his way down the street, we noticed several campers were just in pup tents. "How scary," I whispered, "I hope they'll be all right." When we left the next morning, the garbage cans were back in their places; everyone was fine and fixing breakfast over their campfires. What we had witnessed must have been a common night ritual.

"Sand dunes? What are sand dunes doing in the middle of the desert?" I asked. Sure enough, the high winds had blown mountains of sand along the Sangre de Cristo Range, forming the Great Sand Dunes National Park, and they shone like crystals in the evening sun. The next morning we got up at the break of day to try sliding down these beautiful hills of sand. We had to cross a small stream at first. The water was freezing cold, but armed with cardboard boxes, and kerchiefs across our faces, we waded through.

One Leaf in Time

The sand scrunched and slid as we climbed and climbed. Finally, at the top, we laid down our cardboard sleds and tumbled down the squealing, squeaking sand one after another. What a ride! It was hard to part from this natural roller coaster that day.

Driving into Yosemite, we were greeted by a black bear sitting on the side of the road waiting for a handout. We were cautioned later not to feed the animals as they would start eating everything in sight—even the orange antenna balls that were commonly found on people's cars.

The stately rock formations of granite loomed over the whole park and we strode through fields of lupine, Indian paintbrush, and grasses, following a park ranger as she showed us the different aspects of the park and gave us an interesting talk on the flora and fauna. Towering overhead with sheer granite walls, El Capitan stood, a gray monolith, enticing the rock climbers to attempt an ascent up its slippery face.

Next, Jim drove down the California peninsula to visit Carmel-by-the-Sea. He had heard about the beautiful sands and artists' colonies there. The largest redwood trees ranged on the coast, some big enough to drive a small car through. "It's impossible to see the top of the trees, they're so tall!" marveled Tom. The girls were impressed with the art and airy way of life, which inspired them in later life.

Turning back up Route 40, we drove the hundred miles to San Francisco and Jim's AOA convention. Each child had his or her own little fun-flower duffle bag with convention clothes in it (the boys' bags were denim). As we pulled up alongside the hotel, however, the valet met Jim with, "You can't leave that motor home here. It is too big for our parking lot." What a dilemma. It couldn't be left on the busy street either. Finally, Jim called a camper repair place and told them it needed checking. "Bring it over; but you'll have to leave it all weekend," the manager said, which was just what we needed, as Jim was only going to attend sessions over the weekend and a few days after anyway.

After the convention, which was more or less a working deal, as we were sponsoring a candidate from Northern Virginia to take office as president of the AOA, we headed up to Crater Lake. This large basin of pristine water was formed from the center of a volcano. The beautiful blue of the water reflected the sky and was only replenished by rain, so it was perfectly pure. Framed by fragrant pines, it took on the appearance of a large mirror—a large lake of peace.

The most eventful part of the trip for the children was Yellowstone National Park in Wyoming. We parked in a large, grassy field with several other campers around us. Even so, we were warned immediately not to throw any dishwater or food on the ground because it would attract the grizzly bears. Actually, most of the bears had gone back into the woods, where they could find grubs and berries to fatten up on. The animal we did run into was the moose. It was "rutting" time in the summer and a ranger said a mother moose had kept him up in a tree for hours a few days earlier.

We were hiking through some lodge pine trees one afternoon when John stopped short and put his finger to his lips to make us stop. There in front of us was a large moose with a huge rack of horns, passively munching grass. We could not run, as the lodge pines had fallen like pick-up sticks across the whole area and we could only step over them one at a time. Quietly, we backed up, keeping an eye on the animal as he pulled grass and chewed impolitely, unaware that we were there. Then we ran like crazy.

Visiting the wonderful curiosities of nature was a real experience. We stood and watched as Old Faithful flung hotter-than-boiling water 150 feet into the air. It is supposed to erupt every hour, but sometimes it is thirty minutes late or early. The water spewed into the air on time from its gray mud cone for us. Between 10,000 and 12,000 gallons of water are shot up with each eruption.

Farther along there were pools of hot mud turning and swirling like a bowl full of cookie dough. Green and red algae were actually able to grow in these cauldrons and made a very colorful display.

As we were leaving Yellowstone with its herds of elk and fast-moving longhorn deer, we saw a male bison doing a prairie dance across a grassy field. The kids wanted to get out and take a picture of him, but the way he was humping his back and pounding the ground with his hoofs indicated he was terribly angry. Perhaps he had been chased from the herd or lost his standing to a younger buffalo. Anyway, it was a fitting farewell to a beautiful park.

Next, Jim headed for South Dakota to see Mount Rushmore. The flowers along the way were beautiful. Wild delphinium, daisies, and buttercups pressed against the rustic fences. "Let's stop and get some Kentucky Fried Chicken," I announced.

Climbing the mountain towards Sheridan, Wyoming, the aroma of the bucket of chicken was invading our nostrils when Jim suddenly announced, "This camper isn't running quite right." Sure enough, as soon as we reached the top, Jim couldn't get it to change gears. "Maybe it needs to cool down. Let's just sit here and eat our chicken," he said.

There were a lot of other tourists enjoying the view from the top of the mountain and one nice man crawled under the Apollo and loosened the belts so that the Apollo could be driven but could not be shifted into low gear. "If you drive really slowly, you should be able to get down the mountain, and there is a dealer in Sheridan," he counseled us. As we rolled faster and faster down the mountain, we realized we had not counted on other tourists being on the road ahead of us. Turning a bend, we came on a family sightseeing as they drove down the mountain.

"Get out of the way. We have no brakes!" The kids and I waved our arms and shouted, but the children in the back seat of the car thought we were playing with them and made faces and waved back at us. In the nick of time, Jim saw a wider part of the road and swerved around them. I was pale and shaking and thought afterwards, "I didn't even try to protect the children or belt them in—we were so engrossed in getting the tourists out of harm's way."

We all breathed a sigh of relief as Jim pulled into Sheridan, but it meant staying over at a small motel while the Apollo got fixed. There was a rodeo that day in Sheridan, but unfortunately we had no transportation so we missed it. This scary episode and a flat tire were the only problems we encountered with the Apollo on the whole trip. The next morning we were on the road again.

Mount Rushmore was awe-inspiring. "How those sculptors climbed to such a height is mind-boggling," said Jim. The faces of the four presidents were so real I was a little disappointed we couldn't climb the wildflower-strewn trail to the sheer cliffs and actually touch them. There were Lincoln, George Washington, Thomas Jefferson, and Theodore Roosevelt all looking so stately over the valley, an appropriate tribute to the end of our park tours.

When Theodore Roosevelt first saved the natural parks for us all to enjoy, he did a marvelous thing! Their beauty is astounding and really gives one the feel of the vastness of this wonderful country. The children, Jim, and I will never forget it.

CHAPTER 20
EACH CHILD IS A PIECE OF YOUR HEART

There was a lot of racial tension at the time that John, Sioux, Midge, and Mary were starting school, so we enrolled them in Chesapeake Academy, a private school that had its beginnings in the 1890s. Except for the science program, the children were not happy there. Mary frequently refused to even put her name on her paper because the teacher kept screaming at her. I was called in and had to stand over her until she did her work. It was rumored that the teacher kept a bottle of Listerine in her desk and was often inebriated. The children managed to get to the sixth grade (which was as far as the school's curriculum went anyway), then started back into public school. Tom never did attend Chesapeake Academy, being five years younger than Mary.

Public school was an unhappy time for them at first. The other children thought they were snobs and tended to pick on them. Midge recalls the time African-American classmates rubbed her face in the dirt and made her eat grass while they were out on the playground and the teacher stood by and watched.

Mary had similar experiences, and one morning, feeling enough was enough, she marched to the principal's office where she pounded on his desk with tears streaming down her cheeks and said, "They have torn up my homework, thrown my pocketbook up in the ceiling light, and lifted my skirt. I want to be taken out of this class!"

The astonished principal changed her to a higher group, where she had a hard time catching up for a while but did okay. I was proud and quite surprised at her spunk. Later on, this assertiveness and tenacity helped her through managerial positions in the Taverns at Colonial Williamsburg.

Sioux came home with good grades and graduated an honor student. When she turned sixteen, she left a poem on my mirror written by Margaret

Mead, which basically said "Let go, it's time for me to fly." I returned a poem to her dresser mirror that I wrote as a sequel to Margaret Mead's:

> Tho' I have raised you from a seed
> To grow and fervor from me drain
> There comes a time I must let go,
> And watch you, guided by the wind
> Encounter days of sun and rain,
> To blossom, into field of grain.
> So quickly you have let me know!
> You float where languid breezes blow,
> Till suddenly the way you go—
> I cannot help—the choice is yours.
> The chilling wind, no longer slow,
> Demanding, forces you to pick
> The place to land, and settle quick,
> So you, in turn, a seed may grow.
> When frost has come and I have passed,
> The shadow of this ghost will cast
> An influence on the way you grow.
> You went where I would have you go.
> With pride I watch you sprout and grow
> Enrich and nurture worlds at last!

Sioux was my independent. When she entered the College of William and Mary in 1976, there was a silence that invaded the house. The other girls and I lost the drive that she instilled in us—the cheerleading ribbons (red and white), the cold potato soup, or Vichyssoise, in large pans taking up my kitchen, and the everlasting telephone calls and crowds of classmates making homecoming floats in our basement. We really missed her enthusiasm for life and her ability to get things done.

The following year, Marjorie packed her bags and headed off to Radford College. On her pillow was pinned a note: "Dear Mom," it read, "I have changed my bed and washed the sheets. It is all clean. Goodbye. I love you—Midge." When I read the note, I sat down on her bed and cried. All I could think of was the little girl that had said, "Mommy, let's spread a blanket on the front lawn and have a picnic," and I had replied, "Not now, honey. Mommy's too busy."

"You'll be sorry when I'm gone and you won't have anyone to vacuum for you," Mary threatened as she prepared for Radford College, too. Yes, I was sorry, but it wasn't the housework help that I missed, it was our forays in the kitchen practicing the mashed potato, or doing a mean rendition of "Me and My Shadow" while washing the dishes together. The camaraderie at the dinner table and their bits of conversation, between Jim's TV news, kept me abreast of town gossip. Most of all, I missed being needed by my girls: to plait a braid, help sew a Holly Ball dress, buy their clothes, and listen to their tales of woe, be it a lost boyfriend or a hard test at school.

When Tom got through high school, it was a little easier. First of all, we had a couple of neighbors whose children were terrors. They took pride in tormenting Tom and driving me crazy. His books were taken away from him as he walked home from the bus and scattered into the woods; his brand-new football was stomped on until it burst; and one day I saw him running across the open field in front of our house, arms loaded with school books, while these two older boys drove their car behind him trying to run him over. I was relieved to have him leave the neighborhood and enter Virginia Intermont College. From there, he went on to get his master's degree in photography at Virginia Commonwealth University. Jim and I were really proud.

It was November 15, 1990, when the telephone rang. John's usually snappy voice was low and mechanical. His "What's for dinner?" was exchanged for a somber "Hi, Mom." I knew that something was wrong.

After spending his high-school years at Hargrave Military Academy, John had elected to join the Coast Guard. The quota was met there, so he drove to Richmond and joined the Army. Jim was devastated. He had plans for his oldest son to attend college, perhaps his alma mater, Tufts. To no avail he tried his best to dissuade John from joining the military until he had finished his education. After spending two years in Colorado, John trained as a medic at Brooke Army Medical Center in Texas and stayed on in the Alabama Reserves when his three-year service in the Army was up.

During his time home, John met Ida Kelsey at Rappahannock Community College where they were both taking courses. They fell in love and were married on June 15, 1980, at Christ Church in Irvington, Virginia.

"I have to report to the armory by 6:00 a.m.," he said. "Our Medical Unit [the 129th] is being activated."

One Leaf in Time

Saddam Hussein had been stopping tankers from passing through the Straits of Hormuz and threatening our oil shipments from Saudi Arabia. When Saddam Hussein invaded Kuwait in the fall of 1990, President Bush thought it was necessary for the United States to take action. He began mobilizing forces and creating a coalition of nations to support an armed intervention, Operation Desert Storm, which was launched on January 17, 1991.

"At first I thought it was a rumor," John said, "and the National Guard would remain in the USA to protect the states. But it's no rumor—we are going to be put into active duty."

After activation, John was sent to Fort Rucker in Alabama, where he was trained in chemical warfare, medicines to be used to counteract nerve agents, and navigation. (Saddam was supposed to be using nerve gas and chemicals to fight his adversaries.) Then he received typhoid, yellow fever, cholera, and malaria shots. His poor arm must have been pretty sore.

Two days before John left, he found out Ida was pregnant. He sent us a piece of yellow composition paper on which he had scribbled his "last will and testament." It gave us the sinking feeling that our son was going into war and we couldn't be there to protect him anymore.

On December 1, his unit flew in a C-141 to McGuire Air Force Base, touching down at Fort Rucker, then Fort Benning, Georgia, and finally to Westover Air Force Base. From there they headed to the Middle East, landing first in Spain and then to Riyadh, Saudi Arabia. Uniforms were scarce, so they had to dye their own underwear, socks, and towels the regulation khaki.

Midge heard of her brother's leaving, and when the plane touched down at Westover Air Force base in Massachusetts, she jumped out of the shower, picked up her baby girl, Rachel, and drove to the airport. Running out onto the tarmac, after jumping over the gate, with sopping wet hair and babe in arms, she screamed at the exiting plane, "Goodbye, Johnny, stay safe!" Our children were always very close.

After six-and-a-half months, John returned from Saudi Arabia just in time to see his baby girl, Patricia, born. We had exchanged a timeshare unit in Pensacola so we could be with Ida and cheer her on. Sioux, Midge, Mary, and Tom, who were married by then, came down with their spouses and children and celebrated John's return and Tricia's arrival on August 20, 1991.

While John was in Dhahran, Saudi Arabia, he was watching the SCUD missiles flying overhead when one of them hit their target. The 14th Quartermaster Pennsylvania Detachment, caught unaware, suffered many casualties; twenty-eight members of this unit were killed. John was one of the first on the spot and was awarded the Bronze Star medal for his expertise and bravery.

CHAPTER 21
CONQUERING SPACE AND NUCLEAR THREATS

Wake up, Mrs. Prince. You're back in your room." A rosy-cheeked little nurse pushed my bed into its cubbyhole and clicked on the TV. This had been my fourth D&C (dilatation and curettage) for unusual spotting and as I opened my eyes it seemed hard to focus on the black and white screen. Suddenly I realized that I was staring at the surface of the moon. It was July 20, 1969, and Neil Armstrong, looking very much like the Pillsbury Doughboy in his baggy white spacesuit, boots, and enormous gloves, had just made the journey that no other human being had completed so far.

Alan B. Sheppard Jr. had traveled as the first American to enter space in 1961 and that had been exciting enough, but now we had actually reached a destination!

As Neil bounced around on what looked like gray dust (rather than the green cheese our forefathers had teased us about), I leaned on one elbow in awe, trying to make out the blurry surface. Was it dust? Was it rocks? Or was it just mounds of clay like the soil we find in our backyard? It was mind-boggling to think that a man had flown in a spaceship so many miles to this unknown piece of substance. Somehow I felt uplifted and in a fantasyland! Who would believe?

Then with quiet aplomb, Neil spoke the simple sentence that was heard around the world: "One small step for man; one giant leap for mankind." Wow! What a tremendous step forward for the United States.

Russia had tried all along to compete with us in conquering space. They had a little satellite that circled around the Earth called Sputnik and a poor little mongrel dog named Laika who suffocated from lack of oxygen when her spaceship went into orbit in 1957. I remember the beep, beep, beep coming from Sputnik as the Russians televised a replica of it. Following that there were apes, mice, fish, and even spiders put into space.

Few of them seemed to survive well. Those that did, however, were a big help to scientists in the study of illness and aging.

After forty years, the United States started carrying astronauts into space on space shuttles, such as the *Endeavour*, to an International Space Station, which was used by Russia, Japan, and other countries to study weather patterns and conduct experiments to help humans survive in space. How ironic that what started out as a jostle for supremacy in space could make our countries closer.

We had our mishaps in space also. The space shuttle *Columbia* blew up after liftoff in 1985, and later the space shuttle *Challenger* exploded on reentry over Texas. We were coming home from Hawaii, where we had a condominium for about ten years, when Tom Nolte, who was a special friend and neighbor, came to pick us up. I noticed that he wasn't his usual jovial self and then he hit us with the news—the space shuttle *Challenger* blew up just as it was entering the Earth's atmosphere. Our plane must have been flying near Edwards Air Force Base when it occurred. It was such a strange feeling to think that we were so close and yet unaware of the fate of these seven astronauts.

One of our greatest accomplishments was the launch of the Hubble telescope. Sent into space in 1990, it has given us exciting images of Venus and Mars and terrific information on the clouds and gases surrounding these planets and the terrain and possibility of moisture, which would mean the possible existence of living organisms.

In 1962, the Hubble telescope was just a twinkle in the scientists' eyes as they strove to develop a long-range instrument to bring back pictures of planets long before man was actually able to go into space. They were about to launch it in 1986 on the spaceship *Discovery* when the *Challenger* episode occurred and all space travel was cancelled. Refinements were made and Hubble was finally launched in 1990, on the *Discovery*. Relying on its pictures and data, we may soon send a man or woman to Mars.

An array of highly sensitive telescopes has been set up in California to monitor any sounds or unexplained objects that are detected in the Universe. Ironically, our success in conquering space has highlighted some of the problems we continue to deal with on Earth. While we are trying to detect unexplained sounds or objects in the Universe, far beyond us, we are still unable to solve the problems of the world here on Earth.

In 1984, Richard Viguerie wrote: "Soviet deaths in Afghanistan exceed losses of U.S. troops in Viet Nam. Are the United States and the Soviet Union doomed to either an endless Cold War or needless holocaust?" Ever since the end of World War II, the two countries had been engaged in a struggle for world domination. Russia was madly working its mentally ill and physically deformed people in Siberia to produce as much nuclear fuel as they could. Even prisoners were sent to the frigid north. Communism was spreading like a wildfire and Americans were fighting it—testing not only atom bombs but the more deadly hydrogen bomb.

At Walnut Court, we were following along with the rest of the Americans. I had a spot picked out in the back of our basement with a plan for an atomic shelter pasted on the wall. Canned goods and water were kept handy and mattresses available to cover the windows. Some people even dug holes in the ground where they had living space and food stored. We were informed by the media as to how thick our walls had to be and how far the radiation could carry. All this hoopla also raised the question, "If you had a small space and just enough food to survive, and your neighbor did not, would you have to shoot him if he was trying to join you?" It was a scary time.

During Ronald Reagan's term in office, Mikhail Gorbachev was the head of the Soviet Union and he and President Reagan saw eye to eye on the necessity of toning down the Cold War. In 1987, President Reagan issued a challenge to Gorbachev: "Mister Gorbachev, tear down this wall." The wall he was referring to was the Berlin Wall that had been built by the Russians to contain East Berlin under Communist regime. The president wanted to see if Gorbachev was serious about searching for peace with the West.

Gorbachev did allow the wall to be destroyed and the people of Berlin attacked it with hammers, axes, and whatever else they could get their hands on. He received the Nobel Peace Prize in 1990.

Although East and West were reunited, they stayed the same in differences. The people still lived in their own sections. Some of the Easterners who moved west have now gone back, mainly because housing is cheaper.

We are still worried about threats from other countries around the world. Iran has started producing nuclear fuel, and North Korea, even though their people are starving, was testing missiles over the Pacific— missiles that are supposed to be able to reach Hawaii. As of 2015, war continues in Iraq and Afghanistan, and, though fewer road bombs are taking their toll of our troops, the terrorists are still active, and we are keeping our fingers crossed that they don't get supplies of chemical or nuclear weapons.

Sputnik 1, first man-made Earth satelite, launched by the Soviet Union in 1957.

CHAPTER 22
GROWTH AND CHANGE, GOOD AND BAD

By 1978, our little Lancaster County had swollen to such a size that a hospital was needed to take care of the many retirees that had moved to the Northern Neck to enjoy the rivers and water views. "Jim," I said, "I think I'll take a refresher course and get back into nursing." I had semi-retired when Tom was born, but working for Dr. Broaddus Gravatt had been fun and easy. He was one of the most laid-back men I have ever had the pleasure of working with. So I put on my thinking cap and spent six months brushing up on new procedures. It was hard learning new methods and instruments, such as pacemakers, but I passed with a B, and with Dr. Gravatt's recommendation, was employed in the medical-surgical unit at the Rappahannock General Hospital (RGH) in Kilmarnock.

We were very short-staffed when I first started on med-surg. Often, the director of the RGH had to come and help us pass out medicines. (He was also a nurse.) One day, while pulling a patient up in bed, I pulled my back out. In an instant, I saw stars. The jabbing pain made me unable to straighten up, and I couldn't lift my leg to get out of a car. After a few weeks, it subsided, but when I saw an opening in the OB unit, I switched over there and stayed on until 1992, when I retired from nursing. The babies were easy to lift, and our team was so much fun.

Betsy Bussells scowled at her egg roll as we sat in the Green Dragon restaurant at our Red Hat meeting. "Yes, I remember the Big Drug Bust on May 6, 1984. My dog was sniffing around because of the strangers on the opposite shore of our house and a policeman had to drag him back by the collar. He took a nip of the policeman, too." The rest of the girls had to hear the story.

The case turned out to involve an icon of the Northern Neck we lovingly called "The Towers." Kendall Hall (its official name) was the site of the county's first and largest drug bust: law enforcement officers confiscated marijuana with a street value totaling close to $10 million. The Coast Guard was alerted that Kendall Hall, one of the castle-like buildings in Irvington, was rented by a man from Washington, D.C. He produced $20,000 in cash from the trunk of his car to rent the estate. An alert policeman notified the Virginia Marine Resources Authority and U.S. Customs, who began surveillance of the property from across the creek in March. Lining the walls of one of the rooms with plastic so he could keep the weed dry, the perpetrator waited until, under cover of darkness, at 1:00 in the morning, the forty-six-foot sailboat *Daddy Warbucks* slipped into Carter's Creek. It had sailed all the way from the Virgin Islands.

As soon as the bales of marijuana were unloaded onto the dock, the Coast Guard spotlights lit up the scene, while blaring megaphones instructed the men handling the drugs to surrender. The six men scattered. Some went up the steps they had taped with white reflector tape, some jumped into the water and tried to hide under the dock, and one man climbed into a dory nearby and rowed across the Rappahannock River.

I never realized that I would soon be involved in the details of this complicated case.

"Guess what? I've been summoned to jury duty right after my birthday in May, Jim. Is there any way I can get out of it?" Brandishing the important-looking document, I accosted my poor, tired husband as he came in from work. It wasn't that I didn't feel this was my civic duty and a very necessary part of our judicial system, but facing an experience that I had never had before, and the thought of making a wrong decision that might affect a person's life, frightened me. Making decisions at home was hard enough.

"I don't think so, Sylvia. You are only a part-time nurse and in good health. Now, if you were a doctor or sick, maybe." (After I pulled my back out on med-surg, I transferred to the obstetric department, working part time, where we didn't have to drag 400-pound patients out of bed twice a shift, but it really wasn't enough to count.)

So, bright and early I drove to the Lancaster Court House. We were not aware until then that the case involved one of the men alleged to be involved in the marijuana drug bust. The judge selected us from several interviewed and didn't buy my lame excuse that being a nurse I was definitely against drugs and therefore might be prejudiced. In we marched to the courtroom through a back corridor right in front of the two drug dealers who had turned state's witnesses. How scary! These men were big, surly gangsters, dressed in dirty sweatshirts and jeans, who scowled down at us with hate in their eyes. I shivered as I quickly passed in front of them.

Jeff Schmidt the Commonwealth's attorney produced pictures of the enormous stack of marijuana piled on the dock; the bundles looked like bales of hay. There was *Daddy Warbucks* moored beside the dock. Then we heard the account of a physician from Ohio who claimed he had come to Kendall Hall to attend a cookout. He registered in a motel at Windmill Point, but on the night of the drug bust he was apprehended by the police while he was trying to thumb a ride to Norfolk. We examined this well-dressed man's shoes, which were soaking wet when he was picked up, and the three bottles of medicine he had left behind at his rented room at Windmill Point. His excuse that he had come to Irvington to attend a barbecue was absurd, as no one in that town knew him. Besides, why would he leave his prescription medicines behind and leave in such a hurry? We debated for several days, but finally decided the circumstantial evidence was strong enough to call him "guilty."

When we pronounced the verdict, however, the judge did not seem to agree with us. He pointed to each one of the jury and repeated our names as he asked, "Did you find this man guilty?" It was very scary, because the rogues who had sailed the boat from the Virgin Islands were in the courtroom giving their testimonies. Now they knew who we were.

As the judge issued his sentence, this criminal turned to his wife who was sitting in the benches and said, "Here take my wedding band—I won't be using it. These people have done me a terrible injustice." All I could think of were the tons of marijuana that these people had planned to distribute throughout Virginia and Ohio to our young children. (This man was released after serving only six months.)

Making my way in a daze to the parking lot, I saw two little children playing in the dust behind a large maroon SUV. "Do you think Daddy will be coming out soon?" one asked the other. I felt so sad when I drove home, locking the doors behind me. This well-to-do physician not only tried to ruin other children's lives, but he had ruined his own, for greed. Jim laughs and tells everyone I ran home and hid under the bed I was so scared.

Although the dealing of drugs may have started earlier, this episode seemed to open a Pandora's Box of crime in our area. There were purses snatched in the grocery store parking lot; people were followed by cars to their own homes and robbed; and several homes were broken into by burglars looking for drugs and money to buy them. Teens high on drugs were involved in car accidents and often died, killing other passengers as well. It seemed like a tragedy occurring every time you opened *The Rappahannock Record*.

The inhabitants of our sleepy little communities no longer felt safe walking on the streets at night, leaving their keys in the car or leaving their doors unlocked. Times had changed. The laid-back homey feeling was gone from the Northern Neck.

John, Sioux, Midge, Mary, and Tom all got married in sequence. Then there were grandchildren: John and Ida had Patricia and James Lee; Sioux and Keith had two boys, Zachary and Zane; Midge and Jon had Rachel and Grady; and Mary was married to George. (Five years after her divorce from him, she was married again, this time to Richard Lewis, who was already blessed with two adult children.) Tom married Victoria years later and they had one little boy, Noah.

It was so nice to see the grandchildren growing up. Keith and Sioux brought the boys from their home in Albion, Michigan, every Christmas, and we went through toys and games, their favorite being dinosaurs. They were replicated in rubber, plastic, and wood, and Zack and Zane were always "biting" Grandma with a dinosaur or fighting each other with them.

CHAPTER 23
HURRICANES AND MISHAPS

"A bad storm is brewing in the Pacific and may reach hurricane strength by the time it reaches Hawaii. Residents of Honolulu have been alerted, as it is aiming directly at Oahu."

This was all we heard on the TV before Iniki, with winds reaching 175 miles an hour, veered to the west and hit our treasured little piece of heaven, Kauai.

Of the five timeshares we had bought during the years (I had visions of leaving them to each of the children), the timeshare on the Island of Kauai and the condominium we later purchased there was our favorite. It was a second-floor unit located in Princeville at the Cliff Club Resort. A lanai in front looked over the ocean, and a lanai in back gave you an expansive view of the mountains with distant ribbons of waterfalls. Soft trade winds and scents of plumeria regaled your senses.

On August 18, 1992, what started as a mild tropical wave intensified into a hurricane and hit the western side of Kauai with brutal force. A couple hiking along the Napali coast were almost blown into the ocean when the tree they were clinging to was wrenched from the cliff. They had been camping and did not hear about the storm's approach.

Authorities tried to evacuate tourists off the island, but planes at Lehui Airport were badly damaged, so a lot of visitors had to hunker down. At the Cliffs, everyone was told to get into the inner bathrooms and cover themselves with mattresses.

Luckily most did, but one family thought it would be "cute" to have a hurricane party. The winds, followed by rain, smashed into the large glass doors of one lanai, tore down closet and hall doors and departed through the back lanai glass doors. The hurricane party was soon over.

Another family left their baby asleep in its crib on the second floor loft while they sought cover. They telephoned the front desk for help when they discovered the baby was left behind and the brave office members at the administration building had to form a hand-to-hand chain, fighting the elements, and make their way to the unit to save the child.

There was no electricity or telephone system after the poles were blown down, so, just as in the days of the ancient Romans, runners went from town to town to carry messages. Aid came from several sources. Some towns in Florida, who, on August 24, suffered from Hurricane Andrew themselves, wanted to send volunteers. But the biggest problem was, being a small island, materials were in low supply and container ships were slow; so the plucky Hawaiians rolled up their sleeves and proudly cleaned up the mess. Three huge piles of separated trash were piled on a blown-down sugarcane field. One contained mattresses, bedding, and clothes; another consisted of refrigerators, stoves and sinks; and a third was made up of splintered wood that was shredded into compost.

"Sylvia, we've got to go there and see what we can repair in the unit," Jim said. So, over we flew to Kauai and checked in at the Cliffs in January. To our horror, there was little we could do. The large glass walls had blown in, leaving glass and debris all over. The floor was studded with rusty nails after the carpet had been pulled up, and part of the carpet was draped over the administration building, which was roofless. There were no stores open, no stoves to cook on or lights, and all the furniture, including the bed, was still damp. It was like a third world country—or worse! Uncannily, an eighteen-inch-wide glass vase, shaped like a mauve scallop, survived, as did one of the throw cushions I had made. The closet in the hall was demolished when two heavy entrance doors were ripped from their hinges, but the closet rod hung suspended in midair with about six hangers still in place. How frightening it must have been for the vacationers crouched in the bathrooms while Iniki raged.

It was so depressing to see the Norfolk Island pine trees stripped of their limbs and left as somber black sticks against a bright blue sky, and massive philodendron vines that had hung from the forests—gone.

The poor Hawaiian people bravely covered their broken roofs with blue tarp and shared what supplies were left. It was too much for us to bear. Needless to say, we were on the next plane back to Virginia.

Again in August, but this time in 2005, another strong hurricane formed off the coast of Africa and swept into the Gulf of Mexico. She was named Katrina, but she was no lady. When she hit Mobile, Alabama, and the towns along the coast of Louisiana, the area was flooded so badly that people drowned in their homes. It broke through the levees in New Orleans, and then the putrid water was captured inside walls, causing mold and rot. We watched as people climbed to the peak of a bridge with signs saying, "Help, come get us!" A horrible flashback even today is that of a red-haired old lady sitting in her wheelchair against the wall of the Convention Center, where thousands were stranded. "This woman died from dehydration and exposure." The TV commentator reported in a nonchalant tone as the camera focused on her wrinkled face and bright red hair glimmering in the sunshine.

President Bush flew over the site, but even he was slow to act and send aid. Finally the rescue boats and helicopters saved one after another from their watery perches. Many dogs and cats were drowned, but the ones that were saved from their rooftops were so appreciative that it was uplifting to see them wagging their tails and looking for their masters.

"This is the ten-year anniversary of the mooring of 'Big Mo' where MacArthur signed the articles of peace after World War II," the pilot said proudly. We were flying back to Hawaii in June of 2008, and our condo was back as lovely as ever. "Look down in Honolulu Harbor and to the left you will see the beginning." (The USS *Arizona* still lay in Pearl Harbor, entombed with all her sailors.) "Now, look to the right where the *Missouri* lays anchored. That is the end!"

By 1997, Jim was getting the bug to travel again. He flew to Elkhart, Indiana, to buy a small RV he had seen advertised in the paper. The "Roadtrek" was just right for us and our little cocker spaniel named Joshua.

It had a large bed in the rear, a closet, kitchenette, and toilet in the middle, and four seats in front. Joshua loved to go with us (although the vibration scared him). Perched in his back seat with a safety belt on, he would gaze out the window like a little honey-colored person. His favorite trick was to catch Cheez-Its we threw over our shoulders to him as we traveled. Every time we stopped at a motel or timeshare where they didn't allow dogs, we would fix Josh a bed on the floor and leave him in the Roadtrek until morning. Jim would tell everyone he bought the Roadtrek for Joshua and Joshua never denied it.

Bumping along Route 301 on one of our journeys to the Cape to see Mother, we stopped at a gas station at the intersection. "I've got to get gas," Jim said.

Grasping the opportunity to walk Joshua, I attached his leash and we jumped out of the Roadtrek. It wasn't long before Josh was pulling me behind telephone poles and road signs, sniffing all the good sniffs, and I didn't see Jim get back into the vehicle. When I looked up, all I could see were the two red taillights of the Roadtrek as it turned back onto the highway. "Jim, Jim!" I shouted, running after the Roadtrek. I had no way of reaching him (cell phones were very rare in 1998) so I stood in the middle of the highway, no purse, in a totally foreign part of Virginia with only my little dog and mosquitoes for company. It was getting dark and several seedy carloads of men passed by giving me the "look over."

Jim, meanwhile, was driving through Dahlgren and into Waldorf, Maryland, when he saw a restaurant he thought we could eat at. "Let's stop here, Sylvia," he said over his shoulder. When I didn't answer, he turned around to find that the dog and I were missing. He had been talking to me along the way, thinking I had stretched out on the bed in back.

I had been standing for two hours looking down the road when an angel, sitting in a nearby McDonald's restaurant, decided I must be a person in trouble and called the police. At first, Joshua was reluctant about getting into a squad car and gave the policeman a growl. "You don't know how lucky you are, lady," he said, giving Josh a shove into the barricaded back seat. "There have been seven women molested in this area recently." Then he called his buddy in one of the other patrol cars after I related my story, and they had a good laugh about it.

"I need to go on my patrol, Mrs. Prince, so I'll have to take you back to the police station. What is the number of the license plate and what make is the vehicle?" he asked. I was so tired and hungry I couldn't think of them, but luckily, I could remember my social security number and that the Roadtrek was registered in my name. The policeman radioed ahead to the Maryland police, who located Jim just as he turned back to get me. By then, I had sat another hour on a wooden bench, holding a thirsty dog, with a doped-up teenage girl sitting across from me claiming she had run away from her boyfriend and was found in the Shenandoah Mountains. It was a terrible experience but one to look back and chuckle about. "Gee, Sylvia, I wondered why you didn't answer when I asked you if you were ready to stop to eat!" Jim apologized.

Mom died on January 5, 1999. She had fallen one Thanksgiving, tripping over a large bag of garbage left after the family Thanksgiving dinner. With her usual pluck, she religiously did her exercises and pushed herself to become mobile again, but finally, at the age of ninety-three, Mom looked at Tom as he picked her up from a second fall and said, "I can't fight it anymore." Like a Trojan, she had refused to leave her little home, but this episode forced her into a nursing home, where she died peacefully.

CHAPTER 24

BACK TO WAR

Marilyn Nolte, one of my best friends, lived only a couple of lanes from us. They had moved into their house on the Corrotoman only a few months after we had built our "dream home" on Taylor's Creek. Marilyn was an avid quilter, creating pictures of flowers, birds, and butterflies on immensely large quilts. She won many prizes and kudos for her beautiful work.

"Sylvia, turn on your TV." Marilyn's voice on the phone was urgent. "There's something horrible going on at one of the Twin Towers in New York. A plane just hit it and the top is in flames and smoke." It was September 11, 2001.

I had turned off the TV after Jim left for work. Turning it on, I was just in time to see a large jet plane circle from the back of the second tower and plummet right into the side of the building. Parts of the first tower, along with the second tower, were showering down to the ground, while smoke and dust billowed out from the wounds. Then the TV concentrated on the people dashing from the buildings, horror on their faces, running as fast as they could, some in high heels, flailing arms and legs, just trying to get out of there! They were the lucky ones. One man called his wife to tell her he loved her and knew he was about to die because flames had barricaded his door shut, and he was on a floor too high to jump from.

I ran to the telephone to give the tragic news to Jim, but he had gone to his Warsaw office. Still, I grabbed a small portable TV that we bought for the Roadtrek and dashed into town so the girls at the office could see what was going on, not even remembering that there was no TV jack at the office! It was so frightening to think that we could be attacked on our own soil, in midmorning, in such a bizarre way.

While this was going on, a third plane, United Airlines Flight 93, was being hijacked by three al-Qaida terrorists. They entered the forward cockpit and used a box-knife and a homemade blade to slit the pilot and copilot's throats. Their destination, it is thought, was to crash the airplane, loaded with fuel, into the White House. The thirty-seven passengers were told to stay calm, but Todd Beamer of Cranbury, New Jersey, quietly got some of the other passengers to help him attempt to overcome the Middle Easterners. They had heard from their cell-phone contacts that the Twin Towers had been struck by other planes and realized that these three intended to use their plane as a bomb also. After calling his wife to tell her goodbye, Todd called out, "Let's roll!" It was a true act of bravery. The plane crashed in a field in Pennsylvania, after passengers wrestled with the three terrorists, and all died.

A fourth plane was headed straight at the Pentagon. Mary, our daughter who was on one of her sales trips in Washington, saw it plow directly into the building. She was stunned as she thought how she had been in that building just the week before.

It wasn't long before President Bush visited the site of the Twin Towers. Bullhorn in hand, he vowed that we would retaliate by destroying the terrorists and Saddam Hussein. What the president did not realize was that Saddam had nothing to do with the terrorists. In fact, Saddam hated Osama bin Laden, the leader of al-Qaida.

Members of the United Nations were called in to send experts on chemical warfare and weapons of mass destruction to seek out Saddam's hiding places, but all they could find were some empty shells and trucks that may have had some equipment in them. Of course, we were afraid that sanctions would be placed on Iraq to limit their sale of oil on the world market; Iraq had many oil fields.

We were awakened one morning with pictures of Baghdad on the television. It was a beautiful city with wide paved streets lined with palms and statues and fountains. I couldn't believe my eyes. Rockets and bombs were exploding all over the city, demolishing it piece by piece. President Bush had declared war on Iraq and we weren't even aware it was to happen.

As the shells exploded, we could hear the wail of ambulances and the media explaining they thought they had hit Saddam Hussein as he slept in his palace. "What are we doing?" I thought, as we heard that Americans with relatives in the city had been told, "We think we are safe. Don't worry about us." We were supposed to be the peaceful nation, not the aggressor.

The Iraq war escalated in March 2003. John was called up again to set up a medical unit in Baghdad. We were losing a lot of soldiers by car bombs; many servicemen were maimed or captured. There were three soldiers found floating in the Euphrates River after they were captured and tortured.

On one occasion, John sent one of his buddies on an ambulance to pick up a hurt soldier, and a bomb exploded in the road behind the ambulance, killing his buddy. This memory will torture him the rest of his life. He felt he should have been in that man's place, rather than staying behind because a little child with third-degree burns all over his body was being sent to their unit and needed treatment.

At Christmas, John sent us an e-mail picture of him lying on a cot. Overhead he had strung all the Christmas cards sent from his relatives and the kind people of Kilmarnock and Pensacola. They meant a lot to him. The only other piece of ornamentation was a field radio attached with a long cord from an electric source somewhere outside the tent. It reminded me of the stark quarters we had at Weihsien Camp.

"For God so loved the world that he gave his only begotten son." As the minister said these words that Easter, I could only reflect on my son endangering his life trying to help his fellow man and how much I missed him. Finally, after sixteen months, Johnny came marching home and the whole family was overjoyed.

John and Ida with baby Trish

John's photo of a Scud missile over Dhahran

John at Camp Udairi

OB group at Rappahannock General Hospital
L to R: Dr. Nichols, Laura Goin, Ann Conkle, Val Muroff, Dr. Wineland,
Margaret Jackson, Me, Susan Faith, Ginny Townsend, Donna Clark (missing)
and Della Gray.

Zack with his grandfather at Indian Creek Country Club

Grandchildren: Zachary, Rachel, Zane, Patricia, James, Grady, and Noah

Sylvia Prince

Jim on cleanup duty in Hawaii

Prince family in Hawaii

The American Molder, Albion Michigan (photo by my grandson)

CHAPTER 25
LET THERE BE PEACE ON EARTH
AND LET IT BEGIN WITH ME

We traveled almost every year to exotic places—Britain, Australia and New Zealand, Cancun and Porto Vallarta in Mexico, Italy and Yugoslavia and Alaska in 2000–2005. They were very lovely, but I always ended up sick. In Mexico, it was Montezuma's revenge; in Alaska I ended up with a rotavirus that was going around and had to sit in our cabin aboard the ship looking out the porthole for the whole trip—quarantined. When I was freed, Jim took me ashore at Ketchikan and bought me a lovely tanzanite pendant, so the trip was not a total loss. It was so sweet of him.

In Italy, it was Mussolini's revenge. The day before we were to board the plane back to America, I woke up vomiting. Luckily, the maid came in and, though she couldn't speak English, she realized I needed help and directed Jim to a drugstore where he was given a strong prescription. I was on my way home the next day.

In 2000, we flew to Switzerland and attended the impressive Passion Play in Oberammergau, Germany. Everyone in the play lived in the quaint town, and shops touted religious gifts of beautiful crucifixes, statues of Christ, and paintings of the Last Supper. At the play, the chorus sang in German (which I couldn't understand), so I started losing interest until a little bird flew to the top of the amphitheater and started singing. He seemed to be competing with the choral group, chirping his little heart out with such passion. When the chorus stopped, he stopped, and suddenly flew away. Was it Christ coming back to join in his story?

Our favorite destination was always Hawaii. Of course, going home to New England and visiting the folks on the Cape could not compare to the other vacations, because I rarely got to see my relatives, and it always felt like home, but in 2009, Jim found a timeshare exchange in

Maui (the middle island, I always called it). We had been watching whales as they swam along the coast feeding their young so they could be strong enough to travel on the long journey to Alaska. As I feasted on Maui pineapple and leaned back on a satin pillow, I stuck a large chunk of the sinfully sweet fruit into my mouth and let the sticky, pungent juice ooze out of my lips and down onto my chin. Maui Gold was the best!

Our elected president, Barack Obama, was to take office that Tuesday. Although the inauguration was to take place at noon in Washington D.C., for us it started at 7:00 a.m. due to the five-hour time difference in Hawaii. Sleepily, we watched the TV, the procession of dignitaries and the crowds, like sardines, jamming the Mall.

Mr. Obama, because he had African-American ancestry and ran on a ticket of "change" for America, was overwhelmed with supporters. Even the movie actors and college population supported him. African Americans who had never voted before turned out to support him. His energy gave a boost to the whole country.

In his acceptance speech to the world, Obama included what was almost a threat: "We will extend a hand to you if you will unclench your fist!" This was in reference to the massacres of thousands of people in Darfur and the Congo in Africa, the clashing of Israel and Palestine over the Gaza strip, the constant battle between the Catholics and Protestant groups in Ireland, and the wars in Iraq and Afghanistan.

He talked about the changes made in America in segregation with recollections of his father, who could not be served in a restaurant forty-five years ago because of his color. "And yet," he said, "this is the meaning of our liberty and our creed, why men and women and children of every race and faith can join in celebration across this magnificent Mall, as I stand before you, to take a sacred oath, for the most dignified position in the United States today."

In his final words he stressed, "What is required of us now is a new era of responsibility—a recognition, on the part of every American, that we have duties to ourselves, our nation, and the world, duties that we do not grudgingly accept but rather seize gladly, firm in the knowledge that there is nothing so satisfying to the spirit, so defining of our character, than giving our all to a difficult task." In other words, a new era of responsibility that all Americans need to put their shoulders to.

And then he said, "As we consider the road that unfolds before us, we remember with humble gratitude those brave Americans who, at this very hour, patrol far-off deserts and distant mountains. They have something to tell us, just as the fallen heroes, the soldiers whispering from the graves in Arlington!" Wow, it really stirred my thoughts of patriotism.

While we were at my grandson's graduation in Albion, Michigan, a few years back, a bronze statue called "The American Molder" caught my eye, largely because I found the inscription, written by James Russell Lowell, so poignant. It read: "No man is born into the world of work whose work is not born with him. There is always work and tools to work with, for those who will; and blessed are the horny hands of toil."

This is what I think the president had in mind.

A picture came to mind of a trip we took to Disneyland with two of our grandchildren, Rachel and Patricia. We entered a haunted mansion, a small room decorated with old pictures, furniture, and drapes but no windows or doors. Suddenly, the walls started to slide inward, making our group of about twenty people crush together. At the same time, ghosts were projected coming from the ceiling, which was also descending slowly. It gave me the feeling of being powerless and claustrophobic, wanting to kick out a wall and scream for help. Even though I realized this was all in fun, it made me frantic. At last a side door opened and a corridor emptied all of us into the rest of the mansion.

Obama, with all of his energy, was about to enter a haunted mansion and have all the problems of the world squeezing him and causing him sleepless nights because it is his "toil." I could only pray that he has the strength and wisdom to solve some of them.

A dear minister from our church once wrote, "Pray that we all stop fighting each other." I guess that is all that is left to do in this "era of responsibility" as I float along not knowing what will be around the next bend on this river . . . the stream of time.

About the Author

Sylvia Churchill was born in Tientsin (Tianjin), China, in a prestigious home built by her grandfather, Harry Churchill, Vice Consul of Foochow. Her father also lived in China and was a businessman. In 1941, the Japanese bombed Pearl Harbor and rounded up foreign nationals, putting them into concentration camps. Sylvia and her family spent three years in Weihsien Camp, where they learned first-hand how harsh their Japanese overseers could be. But they also learned what was important in life and to persevere despite the hardships of Weihsien and repatriation to a new country.

At war's end, the Churchills sailed to America and settled in Cape Cod. Sylvia attended Massachusetts General Hospital School of Nursing and married James Rex Prince, after graduating in 1956. They lived in Richmond for three years, then moved to Kilmarnock, Virginia, where they raised their five children. Sylvia worked as a nurse for Doctor Broaddus Gravatt and at Rappahannock General Hospital, while Jim covered the county as the optometrist.

CPSIA information can be obtained
at www.ICGtesting.com
Printed in the USA
FFOW03n1649300516

24419FF